# THE THROWING CIRCLE

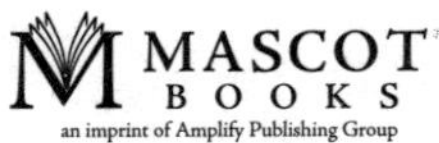


**www.mascotbooks.com**

***The Throwing Circle: Lessons Learned in the Ring about Life, Success, and the Power of Coach-Athlete Relationships***



The author has tried to recreate events, locales, and conversations from his memories of them. In order to maintain their anonymity, in some instances he has changed the names of individuals and places. He may have changed some identifying characteristics and details such as physical properties, occupations, and places of residence.

Cover photo of Luis Rivera at indoor track and field meet in February 2016 courtesy of the Thompson family, Ithaca College, Ithaca, New York.

All interior photos courtesy of the author.

**For more information, please contact:**
Mascot Books, an imprint of Amplify Publishing Group
620 Herndon Parkway, Suite 220
Herndon, VA 20170
info@amplifypublishing.com

Library of Congress Control Number: 2024919607

CPSIA Code: PRV1025A

ISBN-13: 979-8-90026-040-2

Printed in the United States

To my four horsemen—Joseph, Dominic, Santino, and Roman.

# The THROWING CIRCLE

## LESSONS LEARNED IN THE RING ABOUT LIFE, SUCCESS, AND THE POWER OF COACH-ATHLETE RELATIONSHIPS

**CHARLES J. INFURNA, EdD**

# CONTENTS

## PART III: CHASING DREAMS

# FOREWORD

WITH THE 2024 PARIS OLYMPICS RECENTLY COMPLETED, we can soon expect a modest tide of immodest sports books by gold-medal gymnasts, swimmers, and basketball players (and their ghostwriters), inspiring us with their tales of tragedy and triumph, reversal and redemption. And there will be books by the coaches, doling out Great Life Lessons, applicable to business and thus attractive on the lecture circuit.

*The Throwing Circle* is not one of these books, nor is it a manual of athletic technique. It's far more realistic and representative. There's no fame here, much less fortune. Instead, we find the unpretentious memoir of a young coach, working in small colleges, teaching the "throwing sports" of track and field: shot put, discus, and javelin, and the weirdly named "hammer"—a heavy steel ball with a wire and handle, spun around and heaved across a field. These ancient skills, often favoring huge athletes, combine raw muscle strength with the agility and balance of ballet, an exquisite kind of power, but the larger world rarely sees them outside the Olympics.

These athletes and their coaches work almost entirely in obscurity, rarely finding even the fleeting glory that comes to high school football players. They work for the respect and honor of their comrades in the sport. In this way, *The Throwing Circle* is like one of those classic diaries of a combat infantryman in war: no grandiose declarations of purpose or patriotism or high strategy, but only a strikingly honest account of what this physically and emotionally intense, very small world is actually like for its inhabitants. No one dies here, of course, but sometimes their hearts are broken.

Charles Infurna finds himself, as a young graduate student who lifts weights, drafted into working with some "throwers" in the weight room and quickly discovers that he loves the exertion, the training, the challenge of motivating his athletes, the lure of competition, the emotional highs and lows—all the intrinsic satisfactions of athletic competition. He throws himself (so to speak) into it. He coaches for modest pay, in addition to his "real" jobs, while raising a young family. He scratches out the money to go to meets; he somehow finds time to visit with top coaches, some of whom are kind to him. This is not the Olympics. This is how most good coaches actually live.

Initially, though, he's not very good at it, by his own admission. He needs to work at it, as all coaches do, and he improves quickly, which most coaches do not. It's hard to modify your own way of relating to people. But Infurna is both humble and ambitious, a rare mix, and he's willing to change. Step-by-step, carefully journaling his athletes' progress as well as his own, he realizes that fundamental to his success are the individual, particular relationships he has with his throwers. Without mutual trust, he learns, nothing else will happen.

And he does learn this lesson, and then everything else starts tumbling into place. His athletes start making big improvements as he learns who they are and as they come to rely on his judgments. Then he finds a total novice named Luis Rivera, a freshman with no background in throwing, in the college dining hall, and both of their lives are changed. Much of this book is about that story, but suffice it to say that within a few years, Luis, the newbie, has soared to become a Division III national champion in the hammer throw and has come to the attention of Olympic-class coaches. And Coach Infurna has learned a lot about coaching. He and Luis grew in their sport with each other, and readers see it happening in real time.

*The Throwing Circle* is not a book about being a great coach—it's about *becoming* one. That's a very different story, and one well worth reading.

Daniel F. Chambliss
Eugene M. Tobin Distinguished Professor of Sociology, Emeritus
Hamilton College, New York

# INTRODUCTION

When I graduated from SUNY Fredonia in May 2004, I never had any intentions of coaching any sport, let alone track and field. After I graduated from Fredonia, I accepted a job in the fitness center to support myself financially until I could secure a classroom teaching position. When I accepted the volunteer coaching position in November 2004, I did so to help out the team until someone else could. If I had not accepted that position, this book would never have been written. Someone took a chance on me, which essentially set my life on its current trajectory.

As kids, my mom would always tell my brother and me, "You never know. You never know what is going to happen. You never know who is going to walk through that door." She was right. She has always been right. Not until I sat down and reflected on my coaching career did I realize what was going to happen—what my future held. I didn't know who was going to walk through my coaching door.

Unlike NCAA Division I athletics, where scholarships are more readily available, Division III athletics do not offer athletic scholarships. In essence, we can offer academic scholarships to support student-athletes during their time on campus. Since I started coaching in 2004, I thought it would be in my best interest to support any athlete who was interested in competing in track and field. It was a bonus if they wanted to compete in throwing events. Coaches aren't able to peer into the future. We don't have a crystal ball. There might be an All-American or your next national champion walking around your campus who could be seeking a chance, an opportunity.

In 2012 Luis Rivera was that athlete. I had not accepted the volunteer coaching position at Nazareth College yet, but rumor had it that Luis Rivera was discovered in the dining hall. Now I've never coached at any higher level than Division III. You don't often hear of walk-on athletes developing into elite athletes. Every once in a while, you'll see something come across ESPN, but for the greater majority of athletes at the Division I level, the top athletes have already been discovered and offered athletic scholarships. Luis Rivera would not have been discovered at a Division I or even Division II school. He probably wouldn't have been discovered at a Division III school. He was discovered at Nazareth College because he was having lunch in the dining hall with his roommate, who just happened to be a freshman on the track and field team.

If Luis hadn't been having lunch in the dining hall at that moment in time, you wouldn't be reading this book. There wouldn't have been a premise for anything. The stars aligned, as they say, and the coach-athlete relationship between Luis and me began to develop.

Much of what you are going to read in the following chapters centers on relationships. In my case, the coach-athlete relationship I had back then with Luis and continue to have serves as the backdrop for this story. My research in the field of coach-athlete relationships—and specifically the coach-athlete dyad in track and field—has offered evidence that suggests the perceived strength of the coach-athlete relationship from the perspective of the athlete is a strong predictor of athletic success in competition (Infurna, 2023; 2022). Think about that for a moment: the perceived strength of the coach-athlete relationship is directly related to athlete performance. The strength of our relationship propelled Luis toward throwing greatness. Now, I wasn't the only coach in his life who made a positive impact—who was his lightgiver. When Luis transitioned to postcollegiate throwing, Jud Logan, Ashland University head track and field coach, shined a brighter light on Luis than I could. It does indeed take a village.

The premise of this book is focused on coach-athlete relationships. Coaches of any sport and age group of athletes can take the lessons and tools shared here to implement within their own coaching style. The themes I share are of interest and value to coaches of any sport. Understanding your own coaching philosophy as a coach will better assist you in establishing quality coach-athlete relationships. Understanding your values and what is important to you will allow you to share your message with the athletes you work with. Early on in my coaching career, I assumed everyone wanted to be a great thrower. I thought everyone wanted to break records and qualify for nationals. That wasn't the case. It made me realize that I needed to take a deeper look at how I wanted to coach and what was important to me. Soon thereafter, I began sharing my philosophy with my athletes and their parents. I wanted them to know that my top priority was keeping their children safe and providing them with valuable life experiences they could take with them when they graduated. If you want to get better at coaching and want to commit to the critical aspect of building better relationships with your athletes, you could do worse than learning from my mistakes and my successes.

There are many factors that contribute to the success of an athlete. More recent research suggests that the quality of the coach-athlete relationship is the most critical factor that determines an athlete's success (Infurna, 2023; 2022). The coach-athlete relationship—conceptualized as a mutual and causal interdependence between athlete and coach feelings, thoughts, and behaviors (Jowett & Poczwardowski, 2007)—has been the focus of scientific research for over fifteen years (Infurna, 2022; Jowett & Shanmugam, 2016; Jowett & Cockerill, 2003). An effective and mutually beneficial coach-athlete relationship is developed intentionally through a common appreciation and respect (Potrac et al., 2002). There are many factors that contribute to the success of the coach-athlete dyad, such as open communication; establishing rapport, trust, and coach autonomy supportive behaviors; and building credibility (Mageau & Vallerand, 2003; Reznia & Lingham, 2009a; Deci & Ryan, 2000; Infurna, 2022).

Previous researchers have suggested that an effective and mutually beneficial coach-athlete relationship plays a vital role in the athlete's success, and coaches are an important source of support for their athletes (Harry & Weight, 2021; Jowett & Nezlek, 2011; Lafreniere et al., 2011). Similarly, Infurna (2022) showed that coaches who had a clearly defined coaching philosophy and ability to create a nurturing environment also contributed to the success of the coach-athlete dyad with athletes competing at the Olympic and World Championship stage in track and field. Jowett and Chaundry (2004) have shown that positive athlete outcomes, such as team cohesion, may be better predicted by coach leadership in conjunction with the athlete's perception of the coach-athlete relationship. This is consistent with evidence that coach leadership aimed at facilitating positive outcomes for athletes may be conceived of as incorporating both coaching behavior and the improvement of the coach-athlete relationship (Bennie & O'Connor, 2012; Keegan et al., 2014). Qualitative research has demonstrated that positive coach-athlete relationships played a critical role in athlete successes (Infurna, 2022; Bennie & O'Connor, 2012; Gould et al., 2007), student-athlete well-being (Simons & Bird, 2022), and student-athlete mental health (Powers, Fogaca, Gurung, & Jackman, 2020).

This book is broken up into three different sections. In the first section, I share the details that brought me into coaching and my early experiences as a throwing coach at SUNY Fredonia. Reflecting on my 2004–2005 and 2005–2006 seasons, my takeaways are that I learned more of what not to do the next time I would secure a throws coach position. My expectations at the time were that everyone wanted to be great, and everyone wanted to be a conference champion, All-American, or eventual national champion. That was not the case. Far from it, actually. My coaching philosophy evolved from my first season into my second season in many ways. First, I didn't really know what I was doing or how to plan a collegiate track and field season for throwers. I knew what I had previously done as an athlete was not going to work, so I reached out to an unlikely coach who responded to my email and opened my eyes to what coaching could look like and should look like based on the athletes I was working with. With the minor successes I experienced as a coach, I thought my third year would have been the year of exponential growth for my throwers and myself. This section culminates with my termination from SUNY Fredonia via email, which left me doubting myself as a coach.

In the second section of the book, the details shift toward Luis's and my career together at Nazareth College as coach and athlete. We were essentially thrust together, and I was going to coach an athlete who had never thrown before. I learned a lot about myself, my coaching style, and how my coaching style was shaped by the athletes I was coaching. I realized early on in Luis's freshman season that he was going to be a special talent. Rather than trying to fit him into a specific mold, I experienced a paradigm shift in my thinking about how I could better be able to guide him toward accomplishing his goals. I didn't want to force my own expectations on him. Rather, I learned a lot from Luis and how someone with no experience in throwing approached the sport. It was my job to guide him as best I could by illuminating a path for him brighter than he could illuminate for himself, helping Luis develop into the thrower he eventually became—a national champion. I delve deep into Luis's sophomore and senior years in this section. I omit his junior year (because I was not his coach), in which I share the intimate details of what went into that decision and what was best for my family at that time. The section culminates with Luis's senior year—how we came back together, the hardships, the life lessons, the pain, and the accomplishment of Luis winning a national championship during the indoor season and attempting to win an outdoor championship as well.

Finally, the third section details Luis's postcollegiate career. It was when we were sitting in Iowa after Luis won his indoor national championship that I realized the power of coach-athlete relationships and the monumental impact they can have on an athlete's performance. The research behind the science and art of coach-athlete relationships suggests that the perceived quality of the relationship from the perspective of the athlete is one of the most predictive variables that drives athlete success. Once we boarded the plane back to Rochester that March 2016, I knew I needed to learn more about coach-athlete relationships, the power of support systems, and how they ultimately impact athlete outcomes.

# Part I

# AN UNLIKELY COACH

# CHAPTER 1
# NOT IN IT FOR THE MONEY

I GRADUATED ON MOTHER'S DAY, May 2004, from SUNY Fredonia with my BS in childhood education. I was enrolled in Fredonia's curriculum and instruction graduate program, to begin taking courses in August 2004. I was the first person in my family to graduate from college. My parents were proud. I was proud. But I don't believe anyone was prouder than my grandfather Francesco. He graduated with me that day. The sixteen-hour days to take care of my uncle and mom all those years ago were somehow manifesting themselves in Dods Hall on the campus of SUNY Fredonia.

My graduation present from my parents was to spend three weeks in Sicily with my dad's parents. My dad and I flew out after graduation and returned home in the middle of June. It had been a few years since I had last seen my grandparents. Unlike my mom's parents, Calogero and Santa didn't sell and leave everything behind when they first came over in the late 1970s. They would spend a few years in Sicily, then come and spend time with my family or my uncle's, then fly back to Sicily. In middle school and high school, my parents somehow managed to allow us the luxury of spending the summer of 1995 and 1997 in Realmonte, Sicily, where they were both born. These weren't your ordinary vacations. We would leave around the Fourth of July and return to the States the night before school started. I was entering tenth grade in the fall of 1997. I received my schedule that morning and had no idea where I was going. Much like 1997, in 2004, I didn't know where I was going either.

Vacation was amazing. I didn't do much of anything. I would have breakfast with my grandparents, take a walk into town with my grandfather, and watch him and his friends play cards for a few hours. Nonna Santa didn't move around that much back in 2004. We would drive her down to the main street of town, walk to the café, get some coffee, and sit down and watch people carry on with their days. It was a welcome break from what I left back at Fredonia. This vacation would be the last time I saw my grandmother. She lived to the age of ninety-two, and she passed away in February 2007.

When I got back, I thought it would be a good idea to get engaged to the person I had been dating throughout college. It wasn't a good decision, but I thought it was the thing to do. I don't have fond memories of that time. Mostly because this person didn't have similar goals to what I had, and from my perspective, it was a constant battle of doing what I was expected to be doing and what I really wanted to do. We were engaged in July 2004. I called off the engagement in March 2007. We were to be married in July 2007.

Life back in Fredonia during the summer of 2004 was amazing—solely due to my training. I was committed to my goal of qualifying for the 2008 Olympic Trials. I prepared a four-year calendar for myself. I began filling in important dates and meets I wanted to compete in along the way. I decided that in the winter months I would train as hard as I possibly could to prepare my body for the rigors of throwing the hammer in the spring and summer months.

In early August, I was able to find Derek Woodske's email address. I didn't have the courage to email Jud, but I sent Derek a message asking him if I could be considered to join the Ashland Elite team. In my email, I told Derek I was a hard worker, and I would be a valuable contributor to their training group. He replied and politely shared with me that Jud only invited athletes who had met the Olympic standard, but *when* I hit that standard, I would be able to reach out again if I was interested. Reflecting on this moment, I had no business sending Derek a message like this. My personal best in the hammer throw was 48m. The Olympic standard was close to 78m. I had to come close to almost doubling my personal-best throw in that event. He didn't have to respond, but he did. And it was a pleasant response, which gave me hope that I would one day join Ashland Elite.

I hadn't secured a teaching job, but I was able to secure a position in the weight room at SUNY Fredonia. I guess you could say I was responsible for ensuring the weight room was staffed and maintained throughout the day and cleaned at closing. My shift would run from 10:00 a.m. to 3:00 p.m. I would then go to my graduate classes in the evening. It wasn't a bad gig. I was able to train and lift in the morning before my shift started, work and do my homework, and then head to class in the evening. This was the routine I had established for myself throughout the early fall 2004 semester. One afternoon, however, I received a life-changing call.

In late October 2004, while working in the fitness center, I received a call from the AD. "Hi, Charlie, it's Greg. I was wondering if you would be interested in helping out the track team and work with the throwers," he said.

"I can't, Greg. I'm a full-time graduate student and don't have the time right now."

"Well, if you change your mind, give me a call."

The last thing I was thinking about at this point in my life was to be an assistant coach. I was too focused on what I wanted to accomplish that I didn't think I had any time to coach. Greg indicated it would not be a paid position, and that essentially I would be a volunteer coach for the team.

A couple of weeks later, I received a similar call in the weight room. "Hi, Charlie, it's Greg. Are you interested in the throwing coach position?"

"Hi, Greg. I'm not interested. I don't have time to do it for free."

"I think you should really think about it," Greg said.

"Greg, you want me to coach for free. I'm not interested, but thank you for the wonderful offer," I responded.

Shortly after this conversation, Paul Csont came into the weight room. Coach Csont was a staple in Fredonia State track and field. Up until 2004, Coach Csont had been an assistant coach for more than ten years. He was my assistant and the one positive constant in my life as a student-athlete.

"Charlie, just say yes to Greg and coach," he said.

"Coach Csont, I'm not interested in coaching for free. The least Greg could do is offer me a thousand dollars," I said.

"Well, he isn't going to pay you, but I need your help. Come work with our throwers."

"Paul," I said, "I'm not interested. Remember last season? He could at least ask me in person."

Paul walked out of the weight room and returned a few minutes later with Greg. Greg asked me if I would be interested in coaching the throwers for this season, with the possibility of making some money next season. I agreed with the condition that I would be able to travel with and compete at the same meets the team would be competing at. Paul immediately agreed. Greg hesitated for a moment, but reluctantly agreed.

With a few weeks to go before our first indoor meet of the season, I was officially named an assistant coach at SUNY Fredonia, responsible for the throwers.

My fiancée was not happy when I shared the news that the following day I would be spending more time at the track and weight room than usual. She was not a fan of track and field—or training, for that matter. She had not secured a teaching job in the fall of 2004 either. She subbed most days. Other days I would come home, and she would be working on homework or our class projects. We were barely squeaking by with the salary I was making by working in the weight room.

The following day I walked into practice not having any idea what I was getting myself into or what I was actually doing. I had never coached anyone in anything before. I thought I was a good thrower, and also thought that I had figured some things out for myself. But coaching others, not to mention my former teammates, would be more difficult than I initially thought.

On the team were Rob, Wally, Alex, Tim, Jen, and Meredith. Jen and Meredith were my teammates from previous years. Rob was my teammate for one year, left the team, and was now back. Wally was on the team the previous season as well. Tim transferred from Canisius University, outside Buffalo, New York. He was a scholarship kicker on the football team, but when the team dissolved, he transferred to Fredonia and joined the throwing group.

I didn't know what I was getting myself into. I had just agreed to coach my former teammates, transfers, and newbies who had never thrown before. I didn't realize it at the time, but I was probably over my head. With all that said, I don't believe anyone had any expectations for us. Jen was a great thrower. She was probably the best returning thrower in the SUNYAC conference. Meredith could hold her own in the javelin. I wasn't sure about the others. I did know this would afford me the opportunity to continue my own throwing journey. I would have access to the field house and the weight room.

# CHAPTER 2
# WHAT AM I SUPPOSED TO DO?

I WASN'T AS INVESTED AS I SHOULD HAVE BEEN THAT FALL SEMESTER. I was registered to compete in a powerlifting meet in early December and would be missing the first meet of the season to lift with my brother in Philadelphia. I was registered to compete in our home meet the week after our first track meet at Kent State. Rather than spend a lot of time coaching the throwers, I threw myself. I don't remember offering a lot of feedback. I did, however, spend a lot of time coaching Jen.

I wanted to make sure Jen had the best opportunity to defend her discus and hammer championships, as well as try to qualify for both indoor and outdoor nationals. Jen and I didn't have a conversation about goals or qualifying for nationals until we came back from Thanksgiving break. Up until that point in the season, my focus had been to refine everyone's technique, and Jen's was no exception.

Unlike later in my coaching career, a lot of our best conversations came at the Best Buffet in Dunkirk, New York. Usually once a week all the throwers would head over and try to put a dent in the buffet. We would spend the better part of two hours (usually until they closed) trying to clean out the buffet. We came close a couple of times, but it was during these team dinners that I really got to know everyone. You get to know your teammates differently than you get to know them as your athletes. One week before our season opener, I brought a notebook to dinner, and we discussed goals for the season.

I remember sharing my thoughts with everyone about expectations for the season and how everyone would be able to make an impact at our indoor and outdoor conference championships.

"I don't think anyone expects much from us this season," I said. "We have a great opportunity to put SUNY Fredonia back on the map."

The goals we discussed in early December 2004 at the China Buffet ended up spawning an idea for one of my graduate courses later that spring. The goals everyone had for the 2004–2005 season were as follows:

- **Jen**–qualify for indoor nationals (weight throw) and outdoor nationals (discus and hammer).
- **Meredith**–score in the javelin at outdoor SUNYACs.
- **Tim**–score at indoor and outdoor SUNYACs (shot put, weight throw, hammer throw).
- **Rob**–qualify for indoor and outdoor SUNYACs and states in the shot put.
- **Alex**–qualify for indoor and outdoor SUNYACs in the shot put, discus, and hammer throw.

I thought Jen had a realistic chance of breaking our women's weight throw, shot put, discus, and hammer throw school records. Up until this point in Jen's career, she had won ten combined conference championships between the SUNYAC and state meet.

Her technique had started getting cleaned up, and she was now focusing on implementing a three-turn technique with the weight throw. She was a 46' thrower the previous season. She would need to throw close to 52' to have a chance at indoor nationals.

As the first meet of the season quickly approached, I realized that if I was going to be an effective coach, I needed to figure out exactly what I was doing. I wasn't really taking the job as seriously as I should have been. I was taking three graduate courses, kind of had a serious job working in the fitness center, and I was training my heart out to realize my dream as well.

I didn't attend their first meet, because I was competing in a powerlifting meet in Philadelphia with my brother. He was a freshman attending Mary Washington College in Virginia at the time. A friend of his lived in Philadelphia, and he drove my brother up to the meet. We stayed in the same hotel that the competition would

## JOURNALING

Keeping a track and field throwing journal is crucial for several reasons, each contributing to an athlete's journey toward achieving their goals.

First, a throwing journal serves as a repository of invaluable data and insights. By meticulously recording details such as training sessions, technique drills, and competition performances, athletes gain a comprehensive understanding of their progress over time. Analyzing this data allows for the identification of patterns, trends, and areas for improvement, enabling athletes to make informed adjustments to their training regimen and technique.

Second, a throwing journal acts as a motivational tool, documenting not only achievements but also the obstacles overcome along the way. Flipping through the pages serves as a reminder of the athlete's journey, instilling a sense of pride in their accomplishments and fueling their determination to continue pushing toward their goals, even in the face of adversity.

Last, a throwing journal fosters accountability and self-reflection. By regularly documenting their efforts and outcomes, athletes hold themselves accountable to their training commitments and performance objectives. Additionally, reflecting on past entries allows athletes to track their growth, recognize their strengths, and acknowledge areas requiring further development, ultimately guiding their ongoing pursuit of excellence.

In essence, a track and field throwing journal serves as a road map, guiding athletes on their quest for success by providing data-driven insights, fostering motivation, and promoting accountability and self-reflection.

take place. It was our first powerlifting meet. I had no idea what to expect. Neither did my brother.

The powerlifting meet was sanctioned by the USAPL (United States of America Powerlifting) organization. I competed in the 242-pound weight class in the junior category (ages twenty to twenty-three). My brother competed in the 181-pound weight class in the teen III (ages eighteen to nineteen) category. We met up on a Saturday afternoon and competed the following Sunday morning. I didn't have a cell phone at the time, so I wouldn't find out how well our throwers competed until the following day at practice.

We both easily made weight on early Sunday morning. Not knowing what to expect, the meet quickly fell behind schedule. My brother was supposed to first step on the platform at 10:00 a.m. It wasn't until 1:00 p.m. that he began lifting. It was early December, and I knew we had a long drive home back to Fredonia after the competition.

My brother broke two New York State teen III records in the squat and deadlift. I could not have been prouder of him, watching him compete on a platform with some of the best American lifters at the time in the same weight class. I started lifting at 4:00 p.m. I also set two New York State records in the squat and bench press. I also qualified for USAPL junior nationals that upcoming spring. I was thrilled that in my first ever powerlifting meet I had qualified for junior nationals. I have the medals I won that day displayed in my garage gym—a nice reminder of the outcome of all the hard work I had put into training for that competition.

As soon as we started making the trek back to Fredonia, my brother fell asleep in the back seat of my 1996 Delta Oldsmobile. The weather cooperated for me. We were able to make it back to Fredonia from Philadelphia in a little under seven hours. We pulled into my apartment in Fredonia around 5:00 a.m.

# CHAPTER 3
# REACHING OUT TO AN UNLIKELY COACH

I THOUGHT A LOT ABOUT COACHING on the ride back to Fredonia. I thought about the progress some of the throwers had made and what I needed to do to give Jen the best opportunity to qualify for nationals. I wasn't concerned that Jen wouldn't be able to defend her discus and hammer titles. I was concerned that I couldn't coach her well enough to get to nationals. Jen was student teaching, similar to the schedule I had the prior season. I lived in the weight room. Jen stayed away, always telling me that she needed to get her work done and that she didn't have time to lift. This was the first mistake I made as a coach—I treated her differently than everyone else. I didn't hold Jen accountable. I didn't require her to lift. In my mind, I thought that if she quit the team because of something she didn't want to do, I would look bad as a coach and not be asked to come back the following year. I hadn't been coaching for more than a month, and I was already thinking about the following season.

A crazy thought I had on the ride home was to send Jud Logan an email and ask him if I could bring some athletes down to Ashland and watch his athletes practice. It was an idea out of left field, but I knew that if I spoke to the best throwing coach in the country, I might be able to take back some coaching ideas and help Jen reach her goals. During my shift in the weight room that Monday morning, I sent Jud an email. In my email, I told him how exciting it was to have watched him and the other Elite throwers compete at Akron the previous May and that I was training hard in order to qualify for the 2008 Olympic Trials. I wrapped up my email by asking him if I could come down to Ashland and watch him coach for a day. Later on that night, while sitting in class, I received an email back from Jud. In his email, he said I could bring some athletes down to watch a practice and to let him know which day would work for us. After class I sent Jen an IM stating that I had a surprise to share at tomorrow night's practice. I couldn't believe that Jud agreed to let us go down and visit. I knew that a visit with Jud would help put me on the right coaching track.

The following day at practice, I shared the news with Jen and Meredith. The guys had a lab and classes on Tuesday night, so it was only the three of us training on Tuesday nights. We decided on Martin Luther King Jr. Day. Nobody would be on campus yet here in Fredonia, and at Ashland we would be able to watch the Ashland Elite practice in the morning and the collegiate athletes practice in the early afternoon.

That Saturday SUNY Fredonia hosted the Mary Phillips Invitational. It was our second meet of the season, and I would be opening up my 2004–2005 season in my quest toward qualifying for the 2008 Olympic Trials.

The women got things started early on Saturday morning. Meredith hit a SUNYAC qualifying throw in the weight throw. Jen won the weight throw and threw over 50' for the first time in her career. She moved up to number two all time in SUNY Fredonia women's history in the weight throw. She also broke into the top twenty in the nation in the women's 25-pound weight throw. It was a great morning for our female throwers!

Our male throwers also hit SUNYAC qualifying marks in weight throw. Alex and Rob hit personal-best marks in the weight throw. Wally and Tim hit personal-best throws but didn't quite qualify for SUNYACs. I also hit a personal best, throwing 16.28m. I threw about 3' farther than I did the prior season. I was over the moon that I threw that much farther than I did the year before. One of my goals coming into the season was to qualify for USA Indoor Nationals by 2007. I now thought I had a good chance of qualifying in 2006.

We had a strong second meet! All the throwers who competed exceeded my expectations. I still didn't have a clear coaching philosophy and understanding of effective coaching practices, but through two meets our athletes had competed well. Going into the spring semester, Jen was the top-ranked SUNYAC thrower in the weight throw and second in the shot put. Our men were in the top twelve of the SUNYAC conference in the weight throw as well.

My first semester of graduate school went well too. I earned two As and an A–. Much better than where I had left off in my undergraduate program. Nothing had changed academically, but I knew I needed to make up for my poor academic performances as an undergraduate student if I was going to try to secure a teaching job the following fall semester.

I was excited to get back to working with our throwers in the spring semester. I think Coach Csont and Coach Hite (the women's coach) were happy with how our athletes had performed. I didn't share my upcoming field trip with them. I was pretty sure I wasn't

## MENTORS

Reaching out to mentors is essential for personal and professional growth for several compelling reasons.

First, mentors offer invaluable guidance and wisdom born from their own experiences and expertise. By tapping into their knowledge, mentees gain access to insights and perspectives that can help navigate challenges, avoid pitfalls, and capitalize on opportunities. Mentors serve as trusted advisors, providing practical advice and encouragement tailored to the mentee's individual goals and aspirations.

Second, mentors provide constructive feedback and support, fostering a nurturing environment for learning and development. Through mentorship, mentees receive honest assessments of their strengths and areas for improvement, along with actionable strategies for growth. Mentors also offer encouragement and reassurance during times of uncertainty or setbacks, bolstering the mentee's confidence and resilience.

Last, mentors facilitate networking and career advancement opportunities. By leveraging their own professional networks, mentors can introduce mentees to key contacts, provide recommendations, and open doors to new opportunities. Mentors serve as advocates for their mentees, championing their talents and achievements within their respective industries or fields of expertise.



supposed to travel with athletes in my own vehicle, but then again, the spring semester had not yet officially started, so I thought everything would be OK.

Jud and I shared a few more emails before finalizing a date—Martin Luther King Jr. Day 2005. Jen, Meredith, and I drove down in my Delta 88 Oldsmobile. To ensure nobody would find out we went on this trip, I took the E-Z pass off my car. Well, technically it was my parents' car, and all the bills went to their house. I tried being as careful as possible, given the circumstances.

Meredith came over to the apartment complex that Jen and I lived in early that Monday morning. We piled into my car and were off. From the SUNY Fredonia campus to Ashland University is about four and a half hours. It was a cold day, but no snow was in the forecast. I printed off about ten pages of MapQuest directions before we headed out. Jud shared with me that the Ashland Elite team would be practicing in the morning and that the collegiate athletes would be practicing in the afternoon. We were welcome to stay and watch as much as we liked.

The drive down was relatively painless. We pulled into the field house parking lot at around 9:30 a.m. We walked into the field house and couldn't believe our eyes.

# CHAPTER 4
# MY FIRST COACHING MENTOR: JUD LOGAN

STEPPING INTO THE THROWING CIRCLE WAS A. G. KRUGER. He had just represented the United States in the hammer throw at the Athens Olympic Games. Next in line were Derek and Joe Woodske, followed by Crystal Smith. I couldn't believe it.

We quietly walked in, put our gear down away from the circle, and stood in awe for what seemed like an eternity.

"Hi, Coach," I said. "I'm Charles Infurna. Thank you for letting us come down for the day."

"Not a problem at all, Charles. Welcome to Ashland," Jud replied.

Jen and Meredith also introduced themselves. I asked Jud if we could set up a video camera and tape practice. He didn't mind. We set it up a few feet behind the throwing circle and hit the record button. What we recorded hasn't seen the light of day. The only people who have a copy of that DVD are Luis Rivera (I'll go into more detail later), Jen, and myself. I made a few copies of it when we got back to campus later that night. At the time, I had a VHS-DVD recorder-burner. Back then, you had to plug in your camera to the DVD recorder and burn a disc from the camera. I made half a dozen copies when we got back.

We didn't say much to the athletes during practice. It was an amazing experience. AG was an Olympian, and Joe, Derek, and Crystal had represented Canada in international competitions, all throwing the hammer. The more I watched and paid attention to the drills Jud was instructing his throwers to complete, the better I started feeling about myself as a coach. Although my terminology with my throwers was different, the coaching cues were the same. For example, Jud referenced to his athletes that he wanted them to maintain upright posture (back straight, with head and eyes up) while taking turns in the circle with the weight. I would tell our athletes at Fredonia to keep their eyes up by picking something to look at when they were facing the sector at 180 degrees. The cue is essentially the same but worded differently. Jud would also tell throwers to step forward in the circle, meaning when executing the turns to move across the circle in a direction toward the sector (where the implement would be landing). I would tell my athletes to try to bring their foot down at 270 degrees in the circle (close to the same place as moving forward in the circle).

"Coach, how often do you have the Elite athletes complete these drills? They seem too advanced to still be completing drills like this," I said.

"You are never too good to complete drills, Charles. Everything has a purpose. You need to find the right combination of drills that will best help your athletes throw farther," Jud replied. "As you can see, nobody is doing the same thing. AG is working on generating more speed through turns three and four. Derek is throwing a heavy ball. Joe is being Joe, and Crystal is working on getting more comfortable in the circle with four turns. That will help her more when we focus only on the hammer."

"When do you start throwing the hammer in your season?" I asked.

"We throw outside three times a week. We only throw the weight once a week," Jud replied.

"You throw the hammer outside in the winter?" I asked, astonished.

"We throw the hammer all year round, Charles. The college athletes won't throw the hammer until much later in the season. Our Elite athletes focus on the hammer all year round. We only throw the weight because of US indoor nationals," Jud replied.

The concept of throwing the hammer outside all year round was new to me. I assumed that programs would focus on the weight throughout the indoor season and only introduce the hammer in the spring, after the indoor season concluded. I brought my coaching journal with me and wrote down as much as I could from what I heard Jud sharing with the elite throwers.

The elite training session lasted until 11:00 a.m. Derek invited us to lunch and then to observe their lifting training session.

As we sat having lunch with four of the best throwers in the world, I couldn't help but think this wouldn't be possible in any other sport. Jud was a four-time Olympian. AG had just come back from Athens. Derek, Joe, and Crystal had represented Canada in international competition. And there we were, an inexperienced coach who had no idea what he was doing and the two best throwers he was attempting to coach.

Our lunch was filled with lots of conversation, most of which didn't really focus on throwing at all. Derek and Joe shared their experiences training with Jud. Joe was a graduate of Ashland

University, and now he was training as a part of the Ashland Elite group. Derek was not a graduate of Ashland, but at the time was ranked in the top three in the world in the 35-pound weight throw. Crystal was the top-ranked Canadian female weight and hammer thrower. We were sitting in elite company.

I was sitting between Derek and Joe. I didn't feel as though I had much to offer the conversation besides asking them questions about being professional athletes. As part of being on the Ashland Elite team, the throwers were able to live in a house owned by the university free of charge. The university also paid for 100 percent of their health insurance and gave the athletes a meal plan to eat on campus. The athletes had everything taken care of. They each had some side jobs for discretionary income, but the essentials were taken care of. Most importantly, they had the best throwing coach in the United States working with them every day.

After watching their practice and having lunch, we walked back over to the field house to watch their weight-room training session.

As we walked across campus, Derek and I struck up a conversation about coaching.

"Derek, I'm coaching my former teammates. Do you have any tips or suggestions? I'm a little lost," I shared.

"Charles, it seems as though you are doing just fine. You made the trek down here. That shows your athletes that you are committed to their success. Keep showing up and bringing that enthusiasm, and you'll be just fine," Derek replied.

The weight-room session was just as illuminating as the throwing session was. It was like a fantasy camp for throwers. We watched four of the top-ranked throwers spend forty-five minutes crushing themselves in the weight room. What made observing this training session so interesting for me was that there wasn't anything really "special" going on. Squats, clean pulls, and some accessory work. I didn't really know what to expect, but it wasn't that. It was short, intense, and got the job done!

Later that afternoon, the collegiate athletes practiced in separate groups. The female throwers arrived first, spent about an hour and a half training, and then headed off to the weight room. Jud cued his female throwers similarly to the Elite throwers. Common phrases, such as *up-tempo, set the orbit*, and *be long out of the back*, were referenced probably a hundred times. AG was also watching this practice, sharing a thought when required.

"AG, Jud is basically sharing the same cues with the girls as he did when you threw. Once you get to a certain level, that's basically it?" I asked.

"Not really, Charles. Jud cues everyone differently. Some athletes are taller, shorter, faster, and slower. Jud treats each athlete individually. He gives them what they need," AG responded.

As I sat back and watched the rest of the female athletes practice, I took down a bunch of notes in my journal. Jud treated his athletes' technique like an assessment in the classroom. His classroom was the throwing circle. I had been treating everyone the same—the same cues for every thrower expecting different results. What AG said made a lot of sense. I wrote down more notes about treating each athlete differently (in the circle) and programming cues and drills to meet their individual needs. Everyone did pretty much the same thing for the few weeks I worked with our Fredonia throwers. We started with the same drills and the same order expecting different results. Jen, my thrower who had a chance to qualify for nationals, needed something more advanced. Wally, a second-year thrower, required more time with specific drills to fix his technical faults. Meredith needed something totally different because she was a

## DIFFERENTIATING COACHING

Differentiating coaching instruction for track and field throwers is essential for optimizing performance and fostering individualized growth for several key reasons.

First, every athlete possesses unique strengths, weaknesses, and learning styles. Tailoring coaching instruction allows coaches to capitalize on each athlete's strengths while addressing areas for improvement in a manner that resonates with their preferred mode of learning. By adapting coaching methods to suit individual needs, coaches can maximize the effectiveness of their instruction and facilitate deeper understanding and skill acquisition.

Second, differentiating coaching instruction enables coaches to address the diverse range of physical abilities and technical aptitudes present among athletes. Not all throwers will respond to the same cues or drills in the same way, and what works for one athlete may not be as effective for another. By offering personalized instruction based on each athlete's unique capabilities and challenges, coaches can optimize their development and performance outcomes.

Last, differentiation fosters a supportive and inclusive coaching environment that values diversity and celebrates individuality. When athletes feel seen, heard, and valued by their coaches, they are more likely to feel motivated and empowered to reach their full potential. By acknowledging and accommodating the varied needs and preferences of their athletes, coaches can cultivate a culture of trust, respect, and collaboration that enhances overall team cohesion and success.

main-event javelin thrower. It started making sense.

I focused my attention on how Jud interacted with the male throwers. To our surprise, Kibwe Johnson walked in and practiced as well. He was enrolled as an undergraduate student at a local community college and was preparing for the fall 2006 season in anticipation of joining Ashland University's track and field program. I didn't realize he still had eligibility, but then again, he is only a year older than me, so it made sense.

As AG shared, Jud spoke to each thrower differently. The men warmed up with the same three drills that the women did, but then broke up the group and added additional drills. Kibwe threw as well. As I mentioned, Kibwe went on to represent the United States at the 2012 and 2016 Olympics, throwing the hammer. As an undergraduate student, Kibwe would break the all-time collegiate record in the 35-pound weight throw. He would also break the Division II discus and hammer records.

After the male throwers wrapped up their practice, Jud gave Jen, Meredith, and me meal tickets. We ate dinner with the elite throwers and continued our conversation from earlier in the day. As I write this today, I still sit in awe sometimes and think back to this time. Two collegiate athletes and a new throwing coach were having dinner with the best of the best. Another thing that struck me as odd was that nobody bothered us while we were eating.

"I don't want to sound stupid," I started. "But does anyone in the cafeteria know they are sitting five feet away from an Olympian and international athletes?"

"Charles, I think the fame has worn off," AG said with a chuckle. "They know, but nobody is asking for our autographs."

"I'm not going to ask you for one now, but a picture would be nice," I said.

Before we left campus and made the drive back to Fredonia, we had someone take our picture outside the cafeteria with a Kodak disposable camera. We asked for three pictures, just in case we didn't get the right shot the first time.

Our ride home was lively. Besides Meredith falling asleep in the back seat, Jen and I spoke at great length about the remainder of the season.

"Well, Jen, what do you think? I think we need to figure some things out," I shared.

"We have some work to do," Jen replied.

# CHAPTER 5
# DO HOW THE OLYMPIANS DO

Jen and I spoke about her goals for the upcoming season, how she thought she could achieve them, and what she thought I needed to do better this spring to help her get there. I appreciated her feedback on my coaching. I wasn't present at most of the practices, because I was either throwing myself or thinking about the graduate course I needed to get to later in the evening. I realized I needed to be 100 percent present at practice too. I would ask my athletes to be there, but I needed to be there as well. It feels strange sharing this now, but back then I was physically at practice, but not always there mentally.

We discussed the drills we would incorporate into Jen's training sessions. We also decided to introduce hammer drill work as well. With the idea of wanting to qualify for outdoor nationals, we thought it would be best to at least get a hammer in her hands one time per week. Rather than throw the weight three times per week, we would throw two times per week and have a session dedicated to the hammer. I would also have the male throwers do the same thing–focus on the hammer one session per week without

## MAKING THE MOST OUT OF PRACTICE

Coaches play a crucial role in the development and success of their athletes, and staying engaged during practice is essential for effective coaching. Here are two detailed strategies coaches can implement.

1. Active Observation and Feedback Loop
    - Coaches should actively observe their athletes during practice sessions. This means more than just watching; it involves focused attention on the athletes' movements, techniques, and interactions.
    - Create a structured feedback loop where coaches provide timely, specific, and constructive feedback to athletes. This can be done during practice sessions or in one-on-one meetings. Feedback should be tailored to individual athletes' needs and goals.
    - Encourage athletes to ask questions and seek clarification on feedback. This fosters open communication and ensures that athletes understand and can implement the feedback effectively.

2. Utilize Technology and Data Analysis
    - Record practice sessions and review footage with athletes so you can analyze their performances together. This visual feedback can be highly effective in identifying areas for improvement and reinforcing coaching points.
    - Embrace data-driven coaching methodologies by tracking athletes' progress over time. Analyzing trends and patterns in performance data can help coaches tailor training programs

releases. Our net wasn't strong enough to handle the velocity of hammers being released at point-blank range. I didn't think it was appropriate to throw the hammer outside either. We had a gnarly winter, and throwing into three-to-four-foot snowbanks wouldn't accomplish much. Which is funny, because when the indoor season ended, that is exactly what we ended up doing in early March into the beginning of April.

The pace of practice picked up when everyone returned a few days later. We hosted another meet the third weekend in January. Jen broke the weight throw record and also moved up the Fredonia all-time indoor top-ten list in the shot put. Meredith, Tim, and Alex also had really good meets, moving up the SUNYAC list in the weight throw and shot put. I also hit another personal best in the weight throw, throwing 17.26m. Not quite far enough to register for US indoor nationals, but I was getting closer.

The following week a new

thrower joined our group, Nick Lord. Nick transferred from Michigan State, was originally from Central New York, and had never thrown before. I thought this might be a good experiment for the remainder of the season. I began training Nick like I should have started training the other freshmen. We spent a couple of days learning weight throw and hammer technique. After that, practice was all about drills, throws, back to drills, and more throws. Nick must have taken a few hundred turns per training session. Rather than start him with a weight, we gimmicked up an indoor hammer and took tons of hammer throws into the net.

Nick didn't throw especially far during the indoor season, but he ended up becoming a proficient hammer thrower during the outdoor season. Overall, a majority of our male and female throwers had really successful indoor seasons. Rather than write goals focused on qualifying for SUNYACs and states, our throwers focused on

to meet individual needs and optimize overall team performance.

- Since I came back from Ashland University in January 2005, one of the journal prompts I always encouraged my athletes to complete was to track all their distances thrown at track meets. After observing Jud and the Ashland Elite throwers write everything down in their journals, it became very evident to me that the journaling process for this group of throwers was twofold. First, Jud and each thrower were able to maintain accurate distances for each athlete at every meet they competed in. They could refer back to how a week or two or three of weightlifting transitions affected throwing performances. Second—and I told all my athletes this—writing down their distances was meant to act as an additional accountability partner to them. When sharing their goals for the season and writing down a specific number to attain, the journal would act as an additional set of eyes to ensure that actions tracked and the spoken word matched up. Expecting to throw a big distance with the weight, shot put, hammer, discus, or javelin without putting in the work wouldn't prove fruitful. Tracking distances at meets and training sessions would enable us to better plan out weeks when we knew what worked and what may not have worked over the course of a particular training block in relationship to meet performances.

more personal goals. I hadn't figured out process versus outcome goals yet, but I encouraged everyone to not specifically write down distance-based goals. Jen won the 20-pound weight throw at indoor SUNYACs. Meredith set another personal best but didn't qualify for the finals. Bob scored in the 35-pound weight throw and shot put. Nick, Tim, and Alex also threw really well, but not far enough to finish in the top nine and make the finals.

The throwers far exceeded my expectations for the indoor season. Jen wasn't an especially great weight thrower as a junior, but because we made changes to the way she practiced and focused on more technical cues (one or two per meet), she moved up to the top fifteen in DIII in the weight throw. Jen was also the only thrower who qualified for the indoor state meet.

The indoor state meet was the last meet Jen had to move up the nationals list. We knew that the NCAA would take somewhere in the neighborhood of fourteen to sixteen female weight throwers; however, a lot depended on how much overlap there was with the shot put list. For example, if the tenth-ranked shot-putter was also the sixteenth-ranked weight thrower, the NCAA would probably take sixteen weight throwers because they wouldn't be taking an extra individual with that field. They would take the sixteenth person because they were already traveling to the meet anyway. We knew we had six throws left to get where Jen wanted to go.

Jen had a very good indoor state meet. She placed in the top three, but the goal wasn't to win. The goal was to increase her distance and try to move up the nationals list.

When we returned to Fredonia, we had to play a waiting game. There wasn't an ECAC meet to go to that year. We had to wait until after ECACs and the other regional meets finished. We also had to wait for other coaches to submit their athletes' performances and their proof of performance (POP) form. The final entries would come out on the Raceberry Jam website. Jen was sitting at fifteen going into the weekend. She would only go up if some coaches didn't enter athletes, which occasionally happened with middle-distance and distance runners.

On Monday morning, the final list was updated. For the 2005 Division III indoor national championships, it was decided that fourteen women would be throwing the weight. I was devastated.

I spent a good twenty minutes staring at the computer screen. There were some shot-putters ranked after Jen, but taking sixteen or seventeen weight throwers must have been too much for the NCAA that year. I was trying to figure out what to say to Jen at practice later that afternoon. She was at her student-teaching placement, and I didn't think it was a good idea to call her there.

I sat in the weight room that day thinking about what I would say to Jen later that afternoon. I thought about the whole indoor season—what went well, what didn't go well, the time before I started, what could have been. After my shift in the weight room ended, I went up to Coach Hite's office to share my thoughts about Jen and her season. The door was locked. She had already left for the day.

I sent Jen an instant message to meet me at the field house after student teaching. When she walked in, I knew that she knew. I still didn't know what to say.

"Jen, I'm really sorry about how things played out this weekend. Despite not qualifying for nationals, you still had one of the best indoor campaigns of any thrower in Fredonia history," I said.

"All they needed to take was one more thrower. I missed it by a few centimeters," Jen shared.

"I know—a couple of inches. Nobody threw farther this weekend too. I'm really sorry," I reiterated.

We had a nice conversation on the infield of the track. We talked about our trip to Ashland, what we thought went well, and what we thought needed to happen to ensure this didn't happen during the outdoor season. I found it strange that Coach Hite didn't reach out to either of us during the day to share that Jen didn't qualify.

# CHAPTER 6
# GRIT AND PERSEVERANCE

We didn't practice. It would have been our last indoor practice in Fredonia before traveling to nationals. Rather than throw, I gave Jen the day off from throwing. We needed to figure out how to prioritize her outdoor season in order to maximize her time and what would give her the best chance to make nationals in the hammer, discus, or both. We didn't discuss numbers, but we knew it would take at least 50m in the hammer and around 41m in the discus to get there. Jen indicated she wanted to defend both titles at SUNYACs, and attempt to win the shot as well. Her thirty potential points would give the women's team a chance to win as well.

Later that afternoon, when I got back to my apartment, I wrote some thoughts down in my journal. I summarized my thoughts into three categories: what I thought went well, what didn't go as well, and what I needed to work on for the outdoor season to improve my coaching effectiveness. One thing I knew I wasn't going to continue doing was to practice with the team. With the days getting a little longer, and fewer athletes decided to throw outdoors, I had plenty of time to throw after the college athletes were done.

As I was journaling my thoughts, I put in the Ashland DVD and had it play in the background as I wrote. This had become commonplace in my apartment. A couple of nights each week, I would play back and watch the training session we captured in Ashland. Each time I watched, I tried to take something new and apply it to my coaching.

The outdoor throwing team consisted of Jen, Meredith, Tim, Alex, and Nick. Our losses came at the expense of poor grades at midterms, leaving some academically ineligible. My grades were bad, but some of our male and female athletes had such poor grades that without a miracle it would leave them academically ineligible the following fall. So they decided not to compete in the spring and try to save a season of eligibility.

I was beginning to feel better about myself as a coach. I made a lot of mistakes during the indoor season. I tried to coach everyone the same way. I didn't differentiate my programming. Everyone was doing the same thing. To get the best out of the throwers during the outdoor season, I knew I needed to sit down with each person individually and discuss specific goals they had and share them with the rest of the teammates to instill some accountability. I thought everyone wanted to throw far and eventually go to nationals, but that wasn't the case with this team. Everyone had their own definition of *success*.

As had been traditionally completed, the weekend after nationals Fredonia hosted an alumni meet. The times and distances didn't count, and the meet wasn't technically recognized as an official meet, but it was a great way to establish baseline distances and times for our collegiate athletes. In years past, a multitude of alumni throwers competed in the meet. For whatever reason, this season we did not have many at all. I was the alumni thrower who competed that year.

It was a cloudy and chilly day—typical Fredonia weather at the end of March. Each thrower took turns measuring and calling fouls and fair throws. We each all took six throws, same as we would in a regular competition.

Jen and Meredith had really good days. Meredith set a personal best in the hammer and javelin. Jen, working with a new technique, threw close to her personal best in the hammer throw. She didn't have an especially good day in the shot put, but she had a great day in the discus. Nick, in his first outdoor competition of his career, threw the hammer especially well. He came close to hitting 40m, which for a first-time thrower at the Division III level is pretty good. Nick didn't throw the shot put or discus. With the little time we had up to this point in the season, I thought it would be easier to focus on one event and gradually progress with the discus and shot put. I competed as well and set a personal best in the hammer throw. At the time, I

## COACHING JOURNAL

Keeping a coaching journal is indispensable for coaches striving to help their athletes achieve their goals, offering several compelling benefits.

First, a coaching journal serves as a comprehensive record of training plans, strategies, and observations. By documenting coaching sessions, drills, and techniques, coaches can track progress over time and identify patterns or trends in athlete performance. This data-driven approach enables coaches to make informed decisions about adjusting training regimens, refining strategies, and addressing areas for improvement, ultimately optimizing athlete development and performance outcomes.

Second, a coaching journal promotes self-reflection and professional growth. By regularly reviewing their coaching practices and experiences, coaches can identify successes, challenges, and opportunities for growth. Reflecting on past coaching sessions allows coaches to assess their effectiveness, identify areas where they can improve, and set goals for future development. This process of self-reflection fosters continuous learning and refinement of coaching skills, ultimately enhancing the quality of coaching provided to athletes.

Last, a coaching journal facilitates communication and collaboration within coaching teams. By documenting coaching strategies, insights, and feedback, coaches can share valuable knowledge and experiences with their colleagues, fostering a culture of collaboration and innovation. This collective approach to coaching allows coaches to leverage each other's expertise and perspectives, enriching the coaching process and maximizing the impact on athlete development and success.

didn't feel I would have been able to achieve similar success in the discus as well, so I decided to retire from throwing the discus after my senior year. On this day, I was able to muster a throw of just over 53m. I set an unofficial personal best by 4m in what I considered horrible throwing conditions. It was an all-around good start for our throwers.

Our throwers had a strong April. With as many throwers as we had, it wasn't uncommon to have everyone set at least one new personal best in an event. Nick, Tim, and Alex were progressing nicely, especially in the hammer throw. Meredith was finding her stride in the javelin, and Jen had the potential to win the hammer, discus, and shot put at the outdoor SUNYAC championships. Everything seemed to come together on a trip to Slippery Rock at the end of April right before our conference meet.

The year prior our team had the privilege to travel to Slippery Rock and compete. The hammer competition was held on Friday, and after the competition we stayed at the Evening Star Motel. Our administration could not have found a more luxurious location for their athletes than this one. So nice, in fact, that we stayed there on this trip as well. What made this hotel stand out was the monthly, weekly, and daily rates. Nothing but the best for our collegiate throwers.

Jen, Tim, Alex, Nick, and I all set personal-best throws in the hammer competition on Friday night. Meredith was only competing in the javelin the following day, so she was on videotape-recording duty. Jen won the women's competition, and Tim, Nick, and I all made the finals on the men's side. I finished second and extended my personal best by another meter, throwing over 54m.

On Monday morning, after we had returned from Slippery Rock, I was called into the AD's office. Word had spread to some of our throwers' families that we stayed in the hotel we did. I was spoken to about trying to find the most reasonable accommodations for our athletes on such short notice.

"Charlie, we tried our best to find a location for the six of you on Friday," Greg said. "We tried our best."

"You don't have to apologize to me," I shared. "After last year, however, I don't believe the message was well received from this office. The rates of the hotel didn't change, and the meet has been on our schedule since last September. I think we can do better for our athletes."

# CHAPTER 7
# GETTING CLOSER TO THE FREDONIA OF OLD

OUR THROWING SQUAD ROLLED INTO THE OUTDOOR SUNYAC meet with opportunities to score a bunch of points for both the men's and women's teams. The competition took place at SUNY Oneonta, quite a drive from Fredonia. We left late Thursday night and competed on both Friday and Saturday.

On paper the women had a chance to score over forty points. Jen could have won all three of her throwing events, and Meredith was seeded third in the javelin. The men had a reasonable chance to score up to twenty points, which would have almost doubled the points I single-handedly scored the previous year.

Before each meet I would have a brief thrower-team meeting and offer some sage words of advice and thoughts before competition. I always tried to remain as positive as possible given the circumstances of the meet, and always had two or three unique thoughts I'd share with each thrower.

Since our trip to Ashland University, I really took to heart how

## ANXIETY STRATEGIES FOR COACHES

When athletes experience anxiety and overthinking in track and field throwing competitions, coaches play a pivotal role in providing support and guidance to help them overcome these challenges. Here are three strategies coaches can implement to assist their athletes:

1. Establish Precompetition Routines and Mental Preparation Techniques

Coaches can work with their athletes to develop precompetition routines and mental preparation techniques aimed at promoting focus, confidence, and relaxation. This may include visualization exercises in which athletes mentally rehearse their throws, focusing on technique and positive outcomes. Additionally, coaches can teach athletes breathing exercises and progressive muscle relaxation techniques to help them manage anxiety and maintain a calm demeanor during competitions. By establishing consistent routines and practicing mental preparation techniques, athletes can cultivate a sense of familiarity and confidence that helps alleviate anxiety and reduces the likelihood of overthinking.

2. Encourage Positive Self-Talk and Reframing

Coaches can encourage athletes to engage in positive self-talk and reframing to combat negative thoughts and self-doubt. By replacing self-limiting beliefs with affirmations and empowering statements, athletes can shift their mindset from one of apprehension to one of confidence and belief in their abilities. Coaches can also help athletes reframe perceived failures or mistakes as opportunities for growth and learning, emphasizing the

Jud treated his athletes. He made it a point to individualize his coaching to best accommodate his athletes. He was honest and forthcoming, which I think his athletes appreciated. I tried to do the same and not sugarcoat anything for them. I held everyone accountable, but most importantly, they held each other accountable. They weren't afraid to call each other out if someone wasn't living up to the expectations they set for themselves. I reminded them of that before and after each meet. This one, my first outdoor conference championship, was no different.

"What a beautiful day we have," I started. "Not a cloud in the sky. Make sure you put on your suntan lotion so we don't replicate our Slippery Rock incident." Tim and Alex didn't take heed in the past, which left them with a nasty sunburn that was still plaguing them a week later.

"As I've shared in the past, everyone has an opportunity today to reward themselves with the performances they have been working toward. I am extremely proud of everyone and what you have accomplished up to this point in the season. Please reward yourselves with the throws and distances you have earned."

About an hour before the women's hammer competition started, I pulled Jen aside and shared some thoughts with her about the competition.

"Jen, how about this? Nobody probably expected a primary-event discus thrower to be primed to defend a hammer title today, huh?" I shared. "This has been such a special season for you. Everything we've talked about—the goals, going to Ashland, your record-breaking indoor season—this is another wonderful platform for you to showcase your skills for everyone to notice."

"Thank you, Chuck. I don't think anyone is ready for what's to come this weekend," Jen said excitedly.

On the women's side, nobody was expecting the performances Jen went on to have. Jen set a

importance of resilience and perseverance in the face of adversity. By fostering a positive internal dialogue, coaches empower athletes to approach competitions with a mindset focused on success rather than fear of failure.

3. Focus on Process Goals and Controllable Factors

Coaches can help athletes shift their focus away from external pressures and outcomes by emphasizing process goals and controllable factors. Instead of fixating on winning or achieving specific distances, coaches can encourage athletes to set process-oriented goals related to technique, execution, and effort. By concentrating on aspects of their performance they can control, such as their approach, rhythm, and mindset, athletes can redirect their energy toward productive behaviors that contribute to success. Additionally, coaches can remind athletes to stay present-focused and take each throw one step at a time, helping to prevent them from becoming overwhelmed by the magnitude of the competition.

Coaches can assist athletes in managing anxiety and overthinking in track and field throwing competitions by implementing strategies such as establishing precompetition routines, encouraging positive self-talk and reframing, and focusing on process goals and controllable factors. By providing support, guidance, and practical tools for managing anxiety, coaches empower athletes to perform at their best and overcome mental barriers to success.

personal best in the hammer with her first collegiate series (multiple throws) over 50m. She won the competition by 5m. Nobody really had a chance to catch Jen. Either someone was going to have a miracle day, or Jen was going to have to really underperform to be caught.

When it came time to compete, I didn't really speak all that much to my athletes. I never did when I started coaching, and it is something I've continued (or not) to do. Usually, an hour to thirty minutes before the competition, I'd share something positive with each thrower, discuss a cue to focus on, and reiterate the opportunity to reward oneself with a great performance. At nationals, for example, there often aren't a lot of opportunities to speak to your athlete. But I'll get into that later.

Jen picked up right where she left off on day one. Jen finished second, didn't set a personal best, but had three really great throws that showed us she was ready for something bigger next week. The great part about the weekend was watching her chase the shot put championship. As a third event, Jen didn't particularly like the shot put. We would practice the event once a week and not put much thought into her competitions until they really mattered. After finishing second in the discus, Jen was as relaxed as one could be. At the time, I thought she may have been too relaxed to compete, but she set a personal best in the shot put and led right up until the final throw of the competition. Jen unleashed a monster personal-best throw in round five (of six). The final thrower of the competition fouled their attempt in round five. I knew the pressure was on because she was defending her shot put title from the previous season. In round six, the thrower from Oneonta unleashed a throw that surpassed Jen's by about 12cm. Nothing spectacular, but enough for the win.

With Jen's twenty-six total points and Meredith's four points, the women scored thirty points at the 2005 outdoor SUNYAC championships. They were happy, and I was overjoyed to know that in my first year of coaching I had coached a two-time SUNYAC conference champion who was on the verge of qualifying for her first national championship meet. They didn't award a field performer of the meet back then, but if they had, I'm sure Jen would have finished in the top two or three, as far as top scorers go.

My mind was racing on the way back from SUNYACs. I knew Jen had it in her to throw over 51m and all but assure herself a spot at nationals. We had the state meet to focus on next, followed by a last-chance qualifier at Baldwin Wallace.

Taking what I had learned from speaking with Jud at Ashland, he shared with me that he offered his athletes the opportunity to discuss their thoughts about competition. He shared with me that each athlete had a first, second, and third event, and that the athlete's primary focus would be on event one and two, but every once in a while, he would have an athlete like Adriane Blewitt, who won the DII national championships in the indoor and outdoor shot put, 20-pound weight throw, hammer, and discus throw. Those athletes, as he shared with me, were very rare. Just a few years earlier, however, he had two such athletes on the same team who would finish first and second in the 20-pound weight throw, hammer, discus, and indoor and outdoor shot put.

# CHAPTER 8
# BREAKING RECORDS THAT COULDN'T BE BROKEN

WITH WHAT WAS LEFT OF THE OUTDOOR SEASON, I felt it was appropriate to give Jen more flexibility and autonomy with practice and competitions. It started immediately after we came back from Ashland, and as the season progressed, Jen shared more of her thoughts about how things were going and where she wanted to focus her time. Again, I felt this was appropriate for a multitude of reasons, but most importantly, because she was a senior, had achieved a level of success that required a specific skill set to achieve, and had a very good chance at qualifying for nationals. Other throwers on the team shared their thoughts with me about what they wanted to focus on, and we planned their training sessions appropriately. There was never a question about feeling too sore or a lack of motivation to throw. I knew to keep the throwers as engaged as possible with what they were doing, they needed to have a certain

## AUTONOMY

Increasing athlete autonomy is crucial for fostering independence, motivation, and ownership over their training and performance. Here are three strategies coaches can incorporate to promote athlete autonomy:

1. Collaborative Goal Setting

Coaches can adopt a collaborative approach to goal setting, involving athletes in the process of identifying and setting their own objectives. Rather than imposing goals on athletes, coaches can facilitate discussions to help athletes articulate their aspirations, values, and priorities. By actively listening to athletes' input and perspectives, coaches empower them to take ownership of their goals and aspirations. Additionally, coaches can encourage athletes to set both short-term and long-term goals that are specific, measurable, achievable, relevant, and time-bound (SMART). This collaborative goal-setting process not only increases athlete autonomy but also enhances motivation and commitment toward achieving their goals.

2. Providing Choice and Decision-Making Opportunities

Coaches can offer athletes opportunities to make choices and decisions regarding various aspects of their training and competition preparation. This may include allowing athletes to select specific drills or exercises to incorporate into their training routines, choose the order of their workouts, or decide on competition strategies. By giving athletes a sense of control and agency over their training process, coaches empower them to take responsibility for their development and performance outcomes. Additionally, providing

*(continued on next page)*

level of autonomy and say in the direction they wanted their season and careers to go.

The last person who made it to the 2004 outdoor nationals in the hammer threw just under 49m. Jen had already surpassed that distance, but we couldn't be sure that there wouldn't be three or four throwers who went over 50m during the last weekend of competition. Coach Hite thought it would be appropriate for her to attend this meet with Jen and me. I argued that it would be better if just Jen and I went, but Coach Hite didn't like that idea. I thought she was coming more to babysit us than anything else. She hadn't had more than a few conversations with Jen all season. I didn't think there was any reason for her to suddenly be engaged with what was happening now.

We arrived with plenty of time to warm up and get ready for the competition. There were a lot of teams that we hadn't competed against in the past, which was nice. It was a change of pace to compete against some of the Ohio schools. Jen was competing in the second flight of the women's hammer competition. If Jen went over 51m, she would jump into the top ten, all but assuring herself an opportunity to compete at nationals.

"How are you feeling, Jen?" I asked before she started warming up.

"I feel good. Better than I did at SUNYACs," Jen replied. "How do you feel?"

"I feel wonderful," I shared excitedly. "Not a cloud in the sky. A great day to work on my tan," I said with a chuckle.

"You would say something like that, wouldn't you?"

"Whatever it takes to get that hammer to fly farther."

As usual, Jen started warming up when the flight before hers began warming up.

"What are you looking at?" Coach Hite asked me.

"These are the eighth through twelfth ranked women throwers in the hammer throw. As of

choice and decision-making opportunities enhances athletes' engagement, motivation, and intrinsic satisfaction with their training experiences.

3. Encouraging Reflective Practice and Self-Assessment

Coaches can promote reflective practice and self-assessment among athletes to cultivate self-awareness, critical thinking, and self-regulation skills. Coaches can encourage athletes to regularly reflect on their training sessions, competitions, and performance outcomes, prompting them to identify strengths, areas for improvement, and lessons learned. Additionally, coaches can incorporate self-assessment tools, such as performance journals or video analysis, to facilitate athletes' reflection and evaluation of their progress. By engaging in reflective practice, athletes develop a deeper understanding of their strengths, weaknesses, and learning needs, empowering them to take proactive steps toward achieving their goals. Furthermore, coaches can provide feedback and guidance to support athletes' self-assessment efforts, helping them set meaningful goals and develop personalized strategies for improvement.

Coaches can increase athlete autonomy by adopting strategies such as collaborative goal setting, providing choice and decision-making opportunities, and encouraging reflective practice and self-assessment. By empowering athletes to take ownership of their training and performance, coaches cultivate independence, motivation, and accountability, ultimately enhancing athletes' development and success.

yesterday morning, Jen was twelfth. She dropped two places due to the proof of performance (POP) list being updated. Last year they took sixteen throwers. If she breaks into the top ten, I'm one hundred percent sure she'll qualify for nationals," I replied.

"Do you think she can do it?" Coach Hite asked.

"Of course I do. Especially after her state meet performance. Jen has a big 51m-plus throw in her."

"Hopefully, we see that today," Coach Hite replied.

Before I was able to respond, she walked away and started talking to the Baldwin Wallace coach.

Jen took three really nice warm-up throws, all in the 50m range. All she needed was to throw a few centimeters farther, and she would all but guarantee herself a stop at nationals. Throwing far is much easier said than done. She practiced well in the two weeks leading up to the meet.

Jen had a solid opening throw, right about 49m. I knew that throw would get her into the finals and secure three more throws. She looked very relaxed and was carrying herself differently than she had in previous meets.

It seemed as though she had a chip on her shoulder. Maybe to prove something to me, or Coach Hite, or to the other throwers she was competing against. In round two, Jen unleashed a massive 50m-plus throw. I even let out a shout of excitement. I knew that throw would all but guarantee her a slot at nationals.

"Jen, looking really sharp today," I said. "Bring up the tempo in the next round and it's going to fly."

I was thrilled for Jen. I couldn't believe we would be going to nationals. This rush of excitement overcame my whole body. I didn't have high expectations for myself when I first stepped foot on the track back in November to coach. I was happy for Jen and our program. It had been just about a decade since the last female thrower from Fredonia threw at nationals.

"Jen, you are definitely going into the finals. Keep bringing the heat through the finish," I said.

"Have I moved up the nationals list?" Jen asked. "Am I closer?"

"You are really close," I lied. "Keep moving forward in the circle and you will shoot right up the list."

I lied to Jen. I knew she was going to nationals. I didn't want to tell her, because I wanted to make sure she stayed aggressive in the circle and didn't back off. The final POP list wouldn't be released until Monday morning. I didn't know what was going to happen in other parts of the country, so rather than play it safe, we needed to keep pushing.

In round five of the finals, Jen unleashed a throw over 51m. It was a new personal best, and at that point in the season, it moved her to ninth in the country. I couldn't have been more excited for Jen! She had been through a lot with me over the past four years. This was her moment, and I was happy to be a part of it.

Round six wasn't as exciting. It was another throw just under 50m. It didn't matter. We knew we would be going to nationals in Grinnell, Iowa.

"What do you think, Coach Hite?" I asked. "Pretty good day."

"Yes, it was. Jen broke a record I didn't think would ever be broken," Coach Hite replied.

Jen Galvin broke Jen Gall's decade-long women's hammer record by 5'. We were on top of the moon. It was a great day for Jen. It was a great day for SUNY Fredonia women's track and field. I was pumped. I was taking a thrower to nationals. Based on how the season started, the season could have easily gone sideways.

# CHAPTER 9
# WHY CAN'T I GO TO NATIONALS?

ON OUR RIDE BACK TO CAMPUS, all Jen and I spoke about was the week leading up to nationals. Following the previous season's schedule, we would be throwing the hammer on Saturday afternoon—eight days away. We figured out our throwing and lifting schedule. Coach Hite shared that we would be leaving on Wednesday. We would be able to practice in Iowa on Thursday afternoon and early Friday morning. We had everything sorted out.

On Monday morning, I received an email to go visit the AD. I didn't think I had done anything wrong, so I didn't really think anything of it. Maybe I would be receiving a personal congratulations from Greg.

"Charlie, you aren't going to nationals. When fewer than five athletes from one college qualify, the college is only required to send one coach. Penny will be traveling with Jen," Greg said.

I didn't know what to say. I sat in his office for what seemed like a few minutes, but it was probably five or six seconds before I was able to muster a response.

"Are you sure?" I responded dejectedly. "Only Coach Hite will be traveling with Jen? I'm her throwing coach," I said.

"We understand that, but we don't have money in the budget to fly you out and put you up in a hotel. I'm sorry," he said with a sly grin on his face.

I walked out of his office and went down to see Coach Hite. She wasn't in her office. I called her from the men's track office and left her a message.

"Hi, Coach Hite. This is Charlie Infurna. I just spoke with Greg, and he told me that I won't be traveling with you and Jen. Are you able to put in a good word for me? Please send me an email when you have the chance. Thank you."

I met Jen for practice a few hours later. I didn't mention anything to her, because I didn't want to ruin her moment, her focus, and her training.

In between meeting with Greg and practicing with Jen, I found a room outside Grinnell. As long as I had a hotel room for Friday and Saturday night, I figured I would be OK. According to MapQuest, the drive out would take about sixteen hours. I could drive out late Thursday night and get there sometime Friday morning. It would be worth the trip, attending my first national championship with Jen.

Well, the secret didn't last long. Jen met me on Tuesday morning with tears in her eyes.

"Coach Hite told me you weren't coming with us," she said.

"I know. Greg told me yesterday. I didn't want to tell you, because I already made hotel arrangements. I'll drive out and meet you there. I'll miss Thursday and Friday, but I'll be there to watch you throw on Saturday morning."

"But why?" she continued. "Why are they like this?"

"I'm not sure. I thought I would be going anyway. It wouldn't make sense for anyone else to help you there besides me. What's

Coach Hite going to say to help?" I said with a chuckle.

"It's not funny. She doesn't care about me. She doesn't care that I scored the most points for her team the past two years."

"Well, actually, four years because of all those SUNYAC and state championships. Don't forget those early discus titles."

As I imagined, Jen had a horrible practice. Nothing was going well, so I pulled the plug on her training session. She took ten throws. She was all over the place in the circle. Our plan from Saturday was exploding in our faces. We lived in the same apartment complex, and as we were walking back home, Jen shared that she had told her mom what happened.

"I wonder if Greg will change his mind after he speaks with Mrs. Galvin," I said. "It's not a good look to treat the school's national qualifier like this. Especially a few days before nationals."

Later that afternoon, I received a call from the assistant AD. He notified me that the school was going to fly me out with Jen and Coach Hite. I tried thanking him for the opportunity, but he hung up before I was able to say thank you.

## CHAPTER 10

# WHEN PLANS DON'T COME TOGETHER AS EXPECTED

As I reflect almost twenty years later, I'm not really sure what was going on at this time. All the other times I've attended nationals, I was never told I couldn't travel with the team. It really doesn't make sense. Why wouldn't you want the coach and athlete to travel to nationals together? I know I was a difficult athlete to work with last year, but to purposely–I think–do something like this just seemed odd to me.

I got a call from Coach Hite informing me that we would meet at 4:00 a.m. in front of Dods Hall the following morning. Besides some small talk in the car on the ride up to Buffalo, we didn't speak much at all. We went all of Thursday without even seeing each other. Coach Hite would drop us off at the throwing complex and drive off.

We didn't do much of anything on Wednesday. We arrived and went over to the throwing complex. This was legit. There was a coaches box that I needed to stay in during the competition. Jen and I would be able to engage in communication, but not much. This was new to me.

Something happened on Thursday afternoon during our training session. Jen had a great series of throws, most of which went over the 50m line. We had a plan in place to take ten throws on Thursday and another ten on Friday. Just enough to stay loose and focus on solid technique. As Jen was taking off her throwing shoes, a thrower from a Wisconsin school stepped into the circle and unleashed three huge throws over 50m. This particular thrower was seeded immediately below Jen.

"I need to take a few more throws," Jen said with a look I hadn't seen all season. "I need a few more throws."

"I think you are fine. You have a great series of throws. Let's call it and get back at it tomorrow."

"No, I'm not done. I'm taking a few more throws."

Jen ended up taking eight more throws. It was not a good afternoon.

I didn't say much about it. I should have, but I didn't know what to say. Everything we had discussed earlier in the week went out the window. I was frustrated. Not at Jen, but at myself. As I sat in my hotel room that night, all I could think about was why she didn't want to follow the plan and why she didn't trust our plan enough to walk away after ten throws. I knew I did something wrong, but I couldn't identify the problem. I should have been more assertive in sticking to our plan.

We watched the throwing events on Friday, but there was tension between us. I knew I should have said something, but I didn't want to sound confrontational, especially at nationals. I had a bad feeling about Saturday morning.

Things have changed with nationals since 2005. Back then, athletes were randomized into two different flights. Jen went into nationals seeded tenth. I expected the flights to be divided into two flights—the first flight with throwers ranked twentieth through eleventh and the second flight with throwers ranked tenth through first. When we arrived, we saw that Jen would be throwing in flight one. Her meet average of her top-three marked throws was around 48m. A throw of 48m would qualify her for the finals. I didn't expect everyone to throw what got them to the meet. Some throwers were going to drop off—get nervous, lose focus, etc. Others, however, would be fired up and set a personal best.

Jen warmed up really well in flight one. The two top throwers were also competing in her flight. As long as Jen finished within the top four in the flight, she would make finals.

I shared some thoughts with Jen about the season, how proud I was of her, and how excited I was to watch her compete.

"Reward yourself for all your hard work these past four years," I said.

"Thank you," Jen replied.

Jen's first-round throw went around 45m. Not the start we were looking for, but it was a fair throw, and we were in the competition. Jen's body language didn't change much from her first-round throw to her second-round throw. Her second-round throw didn't go much farther. I could see Jen was starting to think about what was happening, but not in a positive way.

"Hey, you look great. Let's settle into the third turn and hit a smooth finish. You'll be great," I said.

I didn't really know if she would hit a good or great throw. I had a feeling it was not going to go that much farther, but I knew I needed to stay as positive as possible. I didn't want Jen to see that I was nervous, but on the inside, my heart was ready to explode. All the work Jen had put into the season was coming down to one throw.

"Let's go, Jen!" I yelled as Jen's name was called for her third throw.

Jen stepped into the circle. As her toes touched the back part of the circle, she took a deep breath. She held her posture for a few more seconds. The judge sitting immediately in front of Jen raised their yellow flag, indicating she had thirty seconds to initiate her throw. She began her winds, which were as smooth as they always were. She stepped into her first turn balanced, second turn balanced, and released a nice-looking throw. The scoreboard read 46.11m (151'3"). It was her lowest recorded best distance of the season. Her average going into the meet was around 48m.

We locked eyes as her hammer was brought back to her. She was walking toward me with tears in her eyes. I didn't say anything. I didn't know what to say.

As we hugged, I told Jen that I was extremely proud of her and everything she had accomplished.

"You are the best female thrower who has ever thrown for SUNY Fredonia. This moment does not define who you are," I said. I don't know where that came from. It just came out.

As Jen walked back over to the thrower's area, I sat down under a maple tree by the throwing cage. I was overwhelmed with what had just happened. So overwhelmed that I began crying as well. It was my fault that Jen didn't perform well. Something happened over the course of the past few days that came between us. All I kept thinking was that Jen didn't trust me. She didn't trust the plan we developed. She didn't trust me as her coach. I didn't know why.

We flew out early Sunday morning. I nearly slept through my alarm. We were to meet at 4:00 a.m. in the lobby to get to the airport in time to catch our flight. I spent a lot of time writing in my journal after we got back from dinner on Saturday night. I filled a couple of pages with thoughts about the meet, the week leading up to the meet, and the final month of the season. Jen had a fantastic season. The one meet we needed to throw far we didn't. Jen threw almost 5m less than her personal best. I thought we had planned everything out, but at the time I didn't know what I had missed. She had all the physical tools, but something happened with her thoughts and confidence when she watched the Wisconsin thrower walk in and crush three consecutive throws.

Jen and I didn't communicate much when we got back to Fredonia. We lived across the apartment complex from each other, but we didn't speak at all before she moved out. Jen was accepted into Ashland University's education graduate program. Earlier in the season, I encouraged her to contact Jud and see if he would have her coach as a graduate assistant. She was accepted, and Jud agreed to let her be a graduate assistant coach. I was jealous of the fact that Jen would be able to train with Jud. But I was excited for her and the opportunity she had to train with and learn from arguably the best throwing coaching in the world. In the two years that Jen spent at Ashland as a graduate assistant, she improved her personal best in the weight throw by almost 5m. She qualified for and threw at the 2006 and 2007 USA indoor national championships. She also improved her personal best in the hammer from 51m to over 60m. I encouraged her to train for the 2008 Olympic Trials, but after the 2007 season, she accepted a high school teaching position. She has been there since and is married with a son.

# CHAPTER 11
# TEACHING, COACHING, TRAINING, AND FREDONIA, OH MY

CHANGE WAS IN THE AIR AS THE 2005–2006 SUNY Fredonia school year got underway. Lots of changes. I was getting ready to defend my graduate thesis that fall. We had a lot of new throwing faces on campus. And I had secured a full-time teaching position at BOCES. Beginning in August 2005, my schedule looked like this: teach, coach, graduate school, throw, train, dinner, homework, and repeat.

My teaching position at BOCES was that of a traveling teacher, with evening programming focused on educating families two nights per week. During a typical week, I would have an evening meeting focused on providing families in various school districts information about the type of program our teaching team would be educating their children on—sexuality. On any given Tuesday and/or Wednesday night, I would be traveling to school districts across Erie, Chautauqua, Cattaraugus, and Allegany counties. Our geographic region consisted of school districts located in the suburbs of Buffalo, down to Ripley on I-90, and east toward Bolivar-Richburg and Cuba-Rushford. Quite a lot of driving.

My evening teaching program was predicated on my class schedule. I was taking two graduate courses that both met on Monday nights. One course was focused on curriculum mapping a specific subject, and the other was called EDU 690: Graduate Thesis. I shared my schedule with Nolan Swanson and Paul in early September, with the understanding that I would be at practice on the Tuesday and Wednesday evenings I didn't have my evening program, every Thursday, and every Friday. Monday was out of the question because of my graduate courses. Nolan was recently hired as the director of track and field, which meant he was considered both the head men's and women's track and field coach. Paul stayed on as an assistant responsible for coaching sprinters, hurdlers, and jumpers (long and triple). I coached the throwers. Coach Hite stepped away from coaching but continued to teach courses on campus.

Meredith was our lone returning senior. She was joined by Tim, Nick, and Alex. Our newcomers on the men's side were Tom and Zack. Julia would be joining us on the women's side. Julia had thrown in high school, with personal bests of 35' in the shot put and 40' in the weight throw. I had spoken to Julia a couple of times the previous spring semester, but I wasn't sure if she would be joining our team. I was pleasantly surprised that she decided to attend SUNY Fredonia.

Our four returning throwers really assisted me throughout the fall semester. They led voluntary captain's practices through September and October. All the interested throwers met one night at the Williams Center to discuss our program, expectations, my schedule, their schedules, goal setting, and how to hold each other accountable. We met for over an hour in one of the meeting rooms on the second floor. I knew my returning group would be able to hold things together when I wasn't at practice. I shared with Nolan and Paul that I believed in the returning throwers and that they would be able to keep everyone else focused when I wasn't at practice. I'm not sure how they felt about it, but that was the only option available to me. I wasn't going to miss my graduate courses. And I certainly wasn't going to miss attending my evening programs. I was leading those sessions, and it was a part of my job. On the bright side, the Athletic Director's department found it in their hearts to offer me $1,000 to be an assistant coach. I had that going for me if the teaching gig didn't work out.

When the season officially started in late October, I made a point of getting to know each of my new throwers as best I could. I shared with my returning throwers that I would be focusing on getting to know everyone because I knew I wouldn't be there that often. It was important for me to establish a positive rapport with everyone.

Our fall training through Thanksgiving break was rather mundane and boring. When I was able to attend practice, I individualized programming for everyone. Julia, Nick, and Tim followed a similar program because they were head and shoulders ahead of everyone else. Julia had taken to my weight throw coaching rather quickly. We had a mock meet before Thanksgiving break, and she threw the weight 45'. I knew we were on the right track with programming. Nick, Tim, and Meredith were making solid progress as well. Midway through the semester, a new thrower joined our group, Garrett Hart. He was coached by one of my former teammates and had solid technique. His dominant hand was his left, but his high school coach taught him how to throw the weight right-handed. He

## DELIBERATE PRACTICE

Deliberate practice is a fundamental concept in athletic development, essential for athletes striving to achieve excellence in their sport. Unlike mere repetition or casual training, deliberate practice involves purposeful, focused, and systematic efforts aimed at improving specific aspects of performance. Here's why deliberate practice is crucial for athletes:

First, deliberate practice facilitates skill acquisition and mastery. By breaking down complex skills into manageable components and focusing on targeted areas for improvement, athletes can systematically refine their technique, increase their proficiency, and achieve mastery over time. Deliberate practice allows athletes to identify weaknesses, address deficiencies, and progressively advance their skills to higher levels of performance.

Second, deliberate practice fosters adaptation and resilience. Through deliberate practice, athletes expose themselves to challenges and obstacles that push them beyond their comfort zones and force them to confront adversity. By embracing the discomfort of deliberate practice and persisting through setbacks and failures, athletes develop resilience, mental toughness, and the ability to thrive under pressure. Deliberate practice teaches athletes to embrace the process of learning and improvement, rather than fixating solely on outcomes or results.

threw the shot put left-handed. A rather out-of-the-box way to teach someone how to throw.

We would travel to Kent State for our season opener. I was excited to compete, but not as excited as our throwers. Nick and Tim were really progressing with the weight and shot put. I thought Nick had a chance to make the finals if everything came together for him. I also thought Julia had a chance to make the finals as well. I shared with the group that my expectation for them as a group was to have everyone qualify for our indoor SUNYAC championship meet.

I drove all the throwers down to Kent State in one of our huge campus vans. The weather was not cooperating with us down I-90, but we made it in plenty of time. I have always been a stickler for being prepared, and I would rather arrive on campus a few hours ahead of time instead of arriving with just enough time.

The women threw first and did not disappoint. Meredith

had a solid day, qualifying for SUNYACs in the weight throw. Julia warmed up really well and had three huge throws in competition. The only problem was that her three throws were all fouls. I attempted to share some thoughts of encouragement with Julia between each throw, but she did not seem receptive to what I was saying. That was a struggle I encountered throughout the whole fall semester. Some sessions Julia wanted feedback on each throw. In other sessions, she didn't want much feedback at all. I wasn't used to that, but I made it a point to be as accommodating as possible for her. Her last throw went out at the 50' mark. As I watched the weight travel outside the sector over the 50' line, I immediately knew Julia was going to have a special career at Fredonia. She didn't seem distressed over her performance. It definitely bothered me more than it bothered her.

Jen, competing as an unattached thrower, won the women's weight throw with a throw over

Third, deliberate practice promotes continuous learning and growth. Athletes who engage in deliberate practice approach training with a growth mindset, viewing challenges and failures as opportunities for learning and development. By seeking feedback, analyzing performance, and adjusting their training strategies accordingly, athletes continuously refine their skills and expand their capabilities. Deliberate practice cultivates a mindset of curiosity, experimentation, and self-improvement, driving athletes to constantly push the boundaries of their potential.

Finally, deliberate practice enhances mental focus and concentration. By immersing themselves fully in the present moment and maintaining a high level of concentration during training sessions, athletes develop mental discipline and resilience against distractions. Deliberate practice trains athletes to sustain their attention, regulate their emotions, and maintain peak-performance states during competition. This mental fortitude and focus are critical for athletes to perform at their best when it matters most.

Deliberate practice is essential for athletes seeking to achieve excellence in their sport. By fostering skill acquisition, adaptation, continuous learning, and mental focus, deliberate practice lays the foundation for athletic success and enables athletes to unlock their full potential.

19m. In her first meet as a postcollegiate thrower, Jen qualified for the 2006 USA indoor national championships. Jen looked like a completely different thrower. Her technique was so smooth in the circle—flawless. And effortless. It was the biggest jump in performance I had witnessed in my career over the course of one season in the weight throw. In less than four months of training with Jud, she added more than a meter a month to her weight throw.

We had four men throwing the weight throw here at Kent State. Alex and Garrett were throwing in round one. Tim and Nick were throwing in round two. I was fortunate enough to be throwing in round three.

Alex hit the automatic SUNYAC mark in the weight, going just over 40'. Garrett missed the mark by about a foot, but much like Jen, his technique looked seamless. He just didn't have the muscle to match his technique yet. Tim and Nick crushed their first meet. Tim set a personal best, throwing over 13m—a huge improvement from the season before. Nick, not to be outdone, unleashed a monster throw of 14.50m. That was an automatic mark for the SUNYAC and state meet. I expected Tim to hit a big throw, but to be honest, Nick's performance surprised me. He hadn't been practicing like he had this big a throw in him, but that is how it goes in track and field sometimes. Looks can be deceiving.

Throwing against an Olympian and would-be Olympian was electric. No meet could top the excitement that Kent State brought, especially when competing against A. G. Kruger and Kibwe Johnson. I seeded myself a little higher than my personal best because I wanted to make sure I would be throwing in the best flight. Not by much, but 50cm can make a world of difference in a competition like this.

As chance would have it, I was throwing immediately after AG. I never thought in my wildest dreams that I would be in this situation, but here I was. Kibwe Johnson was a few throwers after me, as were a handful of Ashland University and postcollegiate throwers. AG fouled his first throw. I hit a small personal best, just under 60'. I was ecstatic. After round one, I was in seventh place, just high enough to make the finals. AG fouled again in round two. I hit another small personal best, just over 60'. It was my first meet over 60'. The excitement of the competition, coupled with Jud hooting and hollering for his athletes, really does make a difference. What I started learning about myself and how to better coach my athletes was how to be able to harness the excitement and find the right recipe for success.

In round three, AG took a safety throw over 75'. He dropped a turn, and rather than take a toe and three heel turns, he took a toe and two, and dropped a bomb. I tried to follow with my own big throw and hit another small personal best.

I went into the finals ranked sixth. It was my first big meet in which I had made the finals. I was sandwiched between one of Ashland's collegiate throwers and postcollegiate throwers. Kibwe Johnson went into the finals ranked first. AG was second. Fireworks ensued in the finals, which saw both Kibwe and AG come close to the 80' mark. Two postcollegiate throwers, a collegiate thrower, and I rounded out the top six.

It was a great weekend of competition for our throwers. We had a slew of personal-best throws in both the weight throw and shot put. I hit another personal best and was creeping up on the USATF qualifying mark for the men's weight throw. Our group of throwers had a lot to celebrate over the semester break. We had all our throwers qualified for SUNYACs in one of the two throwing events. I defended my graduate thesis project a couple of days after we returned from Kent State, and I was getting more comfortable in my coaching role.

# CHAPTER 12
# TORN BETWEEN WORK AND COACHING

OVER THE SEMESTER BREAK, I spent a lot of time thinking about what was missing from my coaching repertoire. I was getting to know my athletes, I asked them a lot of questions about things unrelated to throwing, and I was getting the athletes to start thinking more about throwing. I felt that the throwers understood there was a reason as to why we were doing things, and I encouraged them to ask questions if they weren't sure about something. We had a strong group, and I thought we could make a big mark at indoor SUNYACs in a couple of months.

When our throwers returned from winter break, we picked up with a couple of home meets before traveling to Ohio. Julia hit a big mark in our second home meet of the season, going over 47'. That was a big throw. And to be honest, I wasn't expecting anything like that. She went into the month of February as the top-ranked female weight thrower in the SUNYAC conference. She was ranked third in the shot put. Nick and Tim were progressing just as well. They were both ranked in the top six in the men's weight throw. Nick was close to hitting 50', and Tim was the perfect training partner for Nick.

I still had a wacky work schedule. I had evening programs on Tuesday and Wednesday nights for a few weeks, which caused me to miss a lot of training sessions. I shared my work schedule with Paul and Nolan every week–same with the athletes. I spent a lot of time driving through the month of February. Lots of driving from Fredonia into Cattaraugus County. Nolan didn't really like the fact that I was missing so much practice time. I was able to attend on Monday, Thursday, and Friday afternoons.

He shared his frustration with me in front of the athletes on a Thursday afternoon in early February.

"Charlie, you are missing a lot of practice. Can't you switch your work schedule with someone else?" Nolan said in frustration.

"I really can't, Nolan. It is part of my job. I have to go to at least one program a week. Right now we are short a teacher, and I need to do two. I can't help it," I replied.

"It's not a good look for you. You should try to figure out a different schedule."

"I'll try my best," I was able to muster.

I didn't feel comfortable with what had just happened. I would have rather had the conversation in a private location between just Nolan and me. I spoke to him about it after our practice.

"Hey, Nolan. Do you have a minute?" I asked.

"Sure," he replied.

"Um, in the future, if you need to speak to me the way you did earlier this afternoon, can we have the conversation in private?"

"What's the problem?" he asked.

"What you shared with me earlier this afternoon made me feel uncomfortable in front of the kids. Let's just have the conversation in private next time."

He didn't really reply to me. I thought that was odd.

As we pressed on toward indoor SUNYACs, our throwing group was really coming together. We were going to the China Buffet in Dunkirk on a regular basis. Our typical Thursday evening after throwing and training in the weight room was spent at the China Buffet. It was a great way to get to know everyone, and all the throwers would let their guard down and enjoy each other's company. It was a great way to unwind before traveling on a Friday night or leaving early on Saturday morning.

Indoor SUNYACs was held at Hobart William Smith College. I never understood why, and from asking others, nobody really understood why either. Fredonia would typically host the indoor state meet, but until Brockport opened their new indoor facility many years later, SUNYACs were always held at Hobart.

The female throwers got things started. Meredith hit a personal best in the weight throw in the first flight. Meredith had been flying under the radar pretty much all indoor season because her main focus for the year was the javelin. She didn't have aspirations for a big indoor season, but finishing up her indoor collegiate career with a weight throw personal best was a great way to transition to the outdoor season.

Julia had a great day. She hit a personal best and finished second in the weight throw. Julia didn't really say much at meets. She kept to herself for the most part, and you could never tell she was really amped up to compete. She was a quiet competitor and let her throwing do the talking.

Tim, Nick, and Zack had good days in the weight throw. Nick and Tim both made the finals and scored points for our men's team. Zack also had a personal best in the weight throw, but just missed the finals.

I felt better about this indoor meet than the 2005 meet. I didn't think a lot was expected of our throwers last year, albeit with Jen and Meredith being the only returning throwers who competed the whole season. I expected Jen to throw well last year. I think everyone did. I don't believe anyone thought Julia and Nick would go off in our conference meets this year.

The state meet was at the Rochester Institute of Technology (RIT). Only Julia and Nick qualified automatically for the meet–Julia in the weight throw and shot put. Nick would throw the weight.

Julia hit a personal best just under 50' to finish third. She hit the B standard for DIII indoor nationals. Her throw at this meet is still the Fredonia women's freshmen record in the weight throw. Nick and I were videotaping Julia's throws from behind the circle. When she let go of that fifth-round throw, I couldn't believe my eyes. From where we were standing, it seemed as though it went over the 50' line. She was just shy. In a strong women's field, third place was amazing. To hit the B standard was crazy. I didn't think we would be traveling to another meet the following weekend. To finish her first indoor season like this was awesome!

Nick also finished his indoor season with a personal best in the weight throw. He hit his personal best in round three, ensuring he would be moving on to the finals. Two throwers at states both scored in the weight throw. I felt very good about that. I felt like I was starting to get the hang of coaching collegiate throwers. I was building rapport, and the throwers were performing well. Julia moved into third all time in the women's weight throw at Fredonia. Nick was just behind me in the weight throw, sitting at eleventh all time. I knew he would knock me off the list next year. I had one year left to enjoy having my name on both the men's weight throw and hammer throw all-time top-ten lists.

# CHAPTER 13
# KEEPING THE STREAK GOING WITH JULIA

Our outdoor season went by rather quickly. We didn't host any meets, which was the first time in a long time that Fredonia didn't host an outdoor meet. In the following years, we would host outdoor SUNYACs, but it wasn't to be during the 2005–2006 season.

We made a couple of trips down to Pennsylvania and Ohio in April. Our throwers always seemed to hit their stride in Pennsylvania. We threw at Slippery Rock University, and you guessed it—we stayed at the Evening Star Motel again. Three for three. We must have gotten a really good rate. If it were my decision, I would have never stayed at this place again.

Julia and Meredith had a very strong meet at Slippery Rock. Julia threw in the finals of the hammer and shot put. Meredith made the finals in the javelin. Nick, Tim, and I made the finals of the hammer. I traded facility records with another postcollegiate thrower for a few rounds. He ended up pulling away in the finals, but I was happy with another personal best. I didn't have as much time to train this season as I did the previous one, but I still managed a personal best. It felt strange competing against my own throwers. I didn't steal a spot from my other male throwers, but competing against them was something I started to think about a lot.

I had a lot of conversations with Tim and Nick over the course of the outdoor season focused on goals, holding each other accountable, and how to better push each other in training. Later in the season, before SUNYACs, we traveled to a meet at Nazareth College. Tim got on the bus and was still visibly drunk from the night before. I spoke to Nolan about it after Tim got on the bus, but he didn't seem to care or mind that Tim reeked of cheap beer from the night before. It was 7:00 a.m., and he was still drunk. I encouraged Nolan to leave Tim home. Nolan didn't see it that way.

This decision did not sit well with me. Early on in the season, we had established team rules, and the NCAA had their own set of rules with regards to alcohol, but it didn't seem to matter. Many of our male and female athletes were treated differently this season. Not necessarily because they were better athletes than everyone else either. They seemed to have different rules. It was the first time that a decision like this affected one of my athletes. I was not happy about it.

I was not able to attend our outdoor SUNYAC championships. I was attending a professional development session back at BOCES. The meet was held at SUNY Brockport. The throwers had their best day of the season. Julia won the hammer competition with a personal best just under 50m—another freshman record that still stands today. She also scored in the shot put. Meredith scored in the javelin. Tim and Nick both scored in the hammer throw. I didn't have a cell phone at the time. They were calling my apartment to let me know how things were going. Unlike today, where just about all track meets are live-streamed, we didn't have the technology back in 2006.

In one season, Nick and Tim had made a tremendous amount of progress in the throwing events. Nick had never thrown before, and in two years he had made significant progress in the weight throw, hammer throw, and discus throw. Tim had prior high school throwing experience, but he had never thrown the weight or hammer before. Julia had improved her personal best in the weight throw by 10'. She beat a great thrower from Brockport in the hammer. Fredonia female throwers had won three consecutive hammer competitions. We were on a nice streak.

Before everyone left for the summer, I gave each thrower a binder and a notebook with some quotes and inspirational thoughts. I made the notes personal for each thrower, which was something new I had done. I didn't write personal notes last year, but in my attempt to better develop relationships with my throwers, I handwrote each of them notes—more like a letter—about why I was proud of them and how excited I was to coach them in the 2006–2007 season.

# CHAPTER 14
# MOVING IN A NEW DIRECTION

WHEN OUR THROWERS LEFT CAMPUS, my training really ramped up. I traveled to a few meets in Pennsylvania and Ohio before the Empire State Games tryouts. You never knew who was going to show up, but I figured if I kept throwing over the 55m–57m mark, I had a good chance to make the team. Tryouts were again held at the University of Buffalo. Jesse Doty was throwing. Jesse was a graduate of SUNY Brockport, had qualified for US indoor nationals a couple of times, and still lived in the area. A thrower from UB was throwing as well. I didn't know much about him, but I figured I'd have my hands full because he was a DI thrower. Jesse was already a consistent 65m–68m thrower. He would have to foul out to not make the team. Jesse came close to hitting a personal best. I did hit a personal best and made my second consecutive team!

The Empire State Games were held in Rochester, New York, during the summer of 2006. My mom's parents were able to make the trip to watch. I don't believe they had ever watched me throw in a meet. I was really excited. Another reason why I was excited was because Nick Lord had made the Central team. I was competing against one of my throwers, but in a different situation.

There was a thrower from Long Island who would end up throwing at the 2008 Olympic Trials in the men's hammer throw. He and Jesse were in a league of their own. I felt like I was leading everyone else along in the competition. The Long Island thrower went over 70 feet, a throw that would have placed in the top eight at the USA outdoor national championships. That mark is still an Empire State Games record. Jesse went over 68m. I threw just under 55m and finished third. My first medal in a major track and field competition. My Olympic Games!

The remainder of the summer was dull compared to my Olympic moment. Now that I had a full-time job in Fredonia, I didn't travel home often. That would come in a couple of summers, but for now, I was taking the month of August off from training. I was still lifting in the weight room, but after Empires, I thought it would be a good idea to take some time off from throwing. My body needed some rest. I needed to establish healthy eating and recovery habits. I was twenty-four years old, but from what I had been reading about rest and recovery, I knew I needed to start listening to my body when it was telling me that I needed a break.

It was a couple of weeks before the start of the 2006–2007 season. I had not yet received my coaching contract in the mail, so I decided to take a walk over to Nolan's office to check on my status. He wasn't in his office. Coach Hite wasn't there either. I went to the AD's office to check. I was informed that I would be receiving my letter in the mail within the next few weeks. I sent Nolan and Paul an email inquiring about my status, but I didn't hear back from either of them. A couple of days before the fall semester started, I received an email from Nolan.

It read:

*Charlie,*
*We will not be bringing you back this year. Your lack of communication and inability to attend all of our practices has led us to making this decision. There were times during the season that you didn't notify me or Paul of your whereabouts, causing you to miss practice. Your lack of professionalism in communicating with us has led us to making this decision.*

*Nolan*

I was fired via email.

# Part II

# COACH AND ATHLETE, UNITED

# CHAPTER 15
# LOST AND UNSURE OF MYSELF

To say I was disappointed in myself would be an understatement. I couldn't believe I was fired from a position I thought I was successful at by email. Nolan didn't have the decency to call me and tell me that he was letting me go. What made matters worse was that the following day I checked the Fredonia website to see if they had updated their meet schedule for the 2006–2007 season. What I found was more upsetting than actually being fired. A new coach's face had replaced mine on the track website. A new coach had already been hired. This was late August 2006.

I was slowly beginning to realize that chasing the Olympic dream was crazy and that I really had no business spending all that time trying to accomplish a goal that had really no chance of being achieved. For the past couple of years, I had been telling my athletes that as long as they had a detailed plan on how to move forward with accomplishing their goals, they would give themselves an opportunity to do so. Without a plan, they were setting themselves up for failure. I was staring failure in the face.

One May evening in 2007, I was sitting in my apartment on

Brigham Road in Fredonia and started writing out all the goals I wanted to achieve in my life. I had just finished reading Lou Holtz's book, *Wins, Losses, and Lessons*. Lou Holtz was the Notre Dame football coach from 1986 to 1996. In 1988 Notre Dame won the national championship, and Coach Holtz cemented himself as one of the all-time great collegiate football coaches. Since the first time I finished his book back in 2007, I've probably read it a few dozen times. I'm fascinated by his story and how he rose through the ranks of coaching to reach the pinnacle of the sport and maintain that level of success over a sustained period of time. I didn't realize it at the time, but this book ignited a little spark in the recesses of my mind that wouldn't come to fruition for another ten years.

In getting back to the section I referenced, Coach Holtz lists over a hundred "things" he wanted to accomplish or take part in over the course of his lifetime. He wrote this list while unemployed and serving as a stay-at-home dad to his children.

I started writing. When I refer back to this list now, it reads more like a very long journal entry. I didn't journal at the time; I only kept track of my throwing and weight-room training sessions. I should have written more down—referencing my training journals now is allowing me to write this section more efficiently.

My Olympic dreams were fading fast. We were about thirteen months away from the Olympic Trials, and I had yet to throw what I thought would qualify me for the Olympic Trials in June 2008. I had been sitting around for a few months just taking up space and not taking care of my body. I wasn't enjoying the process of competing and training. Looking back, it felt tedious at the time. It was something to do. But I thought I was good at it, and without coaching, there was this huge void left in my life. Coupled with a nonexistent social life, I thought of a more efficient way to begin pursuing my goals.

Without knowing it at the time, I repurposed my energies into training, but for different reasons. I was training to prove to others—and to myself—that I could be great if I trained hard enough. Hard enough was not going to suffice. It needed to be more fun, still challenging, but purposeful at the same time.

# CHAPTER 16
# COULD I MAKE IT THREE IN A ROW?

I DIDN'T LEAVE MYSELF A LOT OF TIME to train for the 2007 Empire State Games. According to my training journal, I left myself a couple of weeks to train for what turned out to be the most competitive Western division open hammer competition ever! Because of where I was at that point in my life, I had realistic expectations for myself and this competition.

Truth be told, I had the best throwing series of my postcollegiate career and finished in fourth place. I had made the team in 2005 and 2006, and I was left off the team in 2007. The average of my five fair throws was over 57m. I didn't set a personal best, but after not throwing for a few months, my body felt the best that it had felt in a very long time. My parents came to watch and support me, and even in their commentary after throws, I could hear them say I looked happy.

It was a difficult pill to swallow. I finished fourth. In any other year, I would have won or at least finished second. With the top off my Jeep, I drove home from SUNY Brockport feeling accomplished in the fact that after taking the whole winter and spring off I was able to throw just as well as I had thrown the previous year with far less training. Turning my attention to more purposeful practice helped me better focus on what my goals were for individual training sessions. I wasn't left guessing anymore, because I knew what I wanted to do and had laid out a plan.

# CHAPTER 17
# GETTING THE ITCH TO COACH AGAIN

I STILL CONTINUED TRAINING AND THROWING through the fall of 2007. I competed in a couple meets in December 2007, first at Cornell University and then the following weekend at Kent State. I set a personal best at Cornell, then fouled out of Kent State. In the span of seven days I had the best and worst performances of my career. What makes my December 2007 a memorable one is that I began dating Laura Walther. It happened by accident as I wasn't supposed to be on campus that weekend, but our paths crossed in the intramural office located in Dods Hall.

My maternal grandfather had been diagnosed with cancer, and I spent every weekend traveling home to Rochester from Fredonia to spend time with him. On this particular weekend in December, however, I did not travel home. It was the weekend before Christmas break, and I thought to myself that I would be home for a couple of weeks in just a few days.

Tim Miller, one of my former throwers, asked me if I wanted to come to Dods Hall and watch a high school wrestling tournament. While on campus, I was asked to set up the camera system for a basketball game. The system needed to be set up in the intramural office. I went up and noticed the door was open. There Laura sat at the desk. We knew of each other but had never been formally introduced. I introduced myself to her, set up the camera, and asked her if I could take her out later that night. She asked me to pick her up at her apartment later that evening. From that moment forward we were inseparable.

We dated for less than two years before I asked Laura to marry me. I was attending her graduate school commencement with her parents in May 2009 when I asked them if I could ask their daughter to marry me. I didn't know when I was going to do it, but I knew that I wanted to spend the rest of my life with Laura.

We were married in August 2010 and moved back to Rochester from Fredonia in August 2011.

The move back home was great, but there was still this void missing in my life. I had essentially coached for a few years when I wasn't technically a coach at SUNY Fredonia. But it wasn't the same as having my own team. One afternoon, when I was home recovering from triceps surgery, I started looking up all the local college track and field programs, checking to see if anyone in town was looking for a throwing coach. In the summer of 2012, Nazareth College did not have a dedicated throwing coach listed on their team coaching page. I sent the head coach, James Goss, an email. James is still the director of track and field at Nazareth College. I introduced myself, shared my background, and expressed my interest in being a volunteer coach for the 2012–2013 school year.

Later that afternoon, when Laura got home from school, I told her about my interest in coaching again and that I had an interview at Nazareth College in a couple of weeks.

At the time, Nazareth's track and field program was still in its infancy. Primarily focused on distance events, James changed the landscape of the program when he joined two years earlier. The website didn't have any throwers listed on their roster. I wasn't sure who I'd be coaching.

I met James at his office in the middle of July. We spent about an hour discussing track, my coaching philosophy, and what I expected to get out of the program. I shared my experiences from Fredonia—the good and the not so good—and that I was enthusiastic about coaching again. James told me that he had two freshmen male throwers joining the team, and that there would be one returning female senior thrower and sprinter. James shared that one of the male throwers, Brandon, threw on Long Island and had achieved some level of success. The other male thrower, Luis, had never thrown before, but was discovered in the dining hall earlier in the summer while on campus for orientation.

"He has never thrown before?" I asked.

"No. He is roommates with one of our incoming freshman jumpers. He might be a good thrower," James said.

"Sure, he won't have any bad habits. Any that he develops will be on me," I said.

I agreed to volunteer for the 2012–2013 school year.

I waited for the semester to begin before emailing the throwers and introducing myself. I wanted them to establish some semblance of a routine before inundating them with more emails about myself and throwing. I waited until the middle of September 2012 to introduce myself.

Nobody wrote back to me. I expected that, especially since they had never met me. I told them I was excited to be working with them this year and that they could email me or call me if they had any questions before our first team meeting.

In early October 2012, about fifty total athletes filled a small lecture classroom while Coach Goss reviewed expectations and our schedule with the team. He introduced me and the other assistant coaches, one of whom I was familiar with, Tim Giagios. Tim and I competed against each other in high school. I went to Webster, and he went to Gates-Chili. He then competed collegiately at Buffalo State while I competed at Fredonia. He was a sprinter and hurdler, so we didn't compete in the same events. His teams always managed to beat us at meets. It was nice to see that we would be competing on the same team.

After the whole team meeting wrapped up, I asked my three throwers to stay for a few more minutes so I could share our practice schedule, they could share their class schedules, and to exchange contact information. All three throwers were very polite as I asked them to write down some thoughts they had about the upcoming season. I approached the season with almost no expectations, besides hoping to keep everyone healthy and eligible for the whole year. After our quick conversation, Luis pulled me aside to speak privately.

"Coach, I'm really excited to throw for you and the team," he started. "I've never thrown before, but I'm excited to learn."

"Luis, no worries about not having thrown before. It'll be easier to teach you how because you haven't developed any bad habits we need to work on," I said. "Welcome to the team!"

"Thank you, Coach," Luis replied. "I do want to talk about my classes. I'm having some difficulty in one of my science classes right now. I think I want to drop it so I don't lose my scholarship."

"Well, you can drop it, but you have to keep at least twelve credit hours to remain academically eligible to compete. If you fall below twelve, you won't be able to practice or compete," I said.

"I'm taking fourteen credit hours right now. I met with my advisor, and they said I could take a one-credit course to stay at twelve. She said I would be OK," Luis replied nervously.

"Luis, as long as you have confirmation from your advisor it's OK. You only have this week left to drop and add classes. If you do it, please make sure you register for that one-credit course first before dropping the other one."

"My advisor told me I'll be OK. I'm meeting with her later this week to get everything figured out."

"OK. We have practice on Monday. If you can, let me know how it goes before then. Please let me know if I can help you with anything."

And just like that my first conversation with Luis Rivera had taken place. I thought it was strange to wait until so late in the drop-add week of the semester to make a change like this. He assured me that his advisor was going to help him with everything.

Later that night, I gave my wife, Laura, some highlights of the meeting. I remember sharing with her that I had a bad feeling about that one course that needed to be dropped. The other information I shared with Laura was that Luis carried himself differently than the other athletes in the room.

"Laura, remember when I shared with you that one of the throwers on the team has never thrown before?"

"I vaguely remember," Laura responded.

"I think he is going to end up being the best thrower on the team. He has this certain way about him. He carries himself differently than the other athletes on the team. It's like he has a chip on his shoulder, and he hasn't even competed yet," I said.

"How can you tell that already?" Laura asked quizzically.

"You know how during football games the commentators

sometimes say certain players have that 'it' factor? The intangible characteristic that is difficult to describe, but the best athletes have it. I think he has it."

"You can tell that he has 'it' from one conversation?"

"I think so. As long as he is able to register for a one-credit class, we'll see how the fall semester goes."

## CHAPTER 18

# BE PURPOSEFUL ABOUT WHERE YOU WANT TO GO AND WHY

THE FIRST PRACTICE OF THE 2012–2013 season was scheduled for the last Monday in October. I wanted to make sure I was there before the athletes, so I arrived fifteen minutes early. James was getting some mats ready for practice as I walked in.

I introduced myself more formally to some of the other athletes on the team as I waited for our throwers to arrive. Jess was a physical therapy major, and her schedule was jam-packed with classes. Brandon hadn't decided what his major was—yet. Luis was a business major.

At 4:00 p.m. on the dot, both Brandon and Luis walked in. There was something about them that I couldn't put my finger on so early in the season. From what Jess had shared with me via text message, my understanding was that they liked going out during the week together and would train in the weight room at the same time, but

## GOAL-SETTING

Process versus Outcome Goals

There are two types of goals that you may set for yourself this upcoming season. The first type of goal you may decide to pursue is an outcome goal. An outcome goal is fixed, concrete, and has a number or specific result attached to it.

A second type of goal that your athlete may decide to pursue is called a process goal. A process goal is more focused on what you need to do in order to achieve your outcome goal. Process goals are 100 percent in your control. Focusing on process goals will help reduce your stress and anxiety during the course of a season because they are outcomes and results that are directly in your control. Process goals are actionable and leave you 100 percent accountable for the outcome(s) you are seeking.

Step 1: List one or two goals. What do you want to accomplish? What do you aspire to achieve? Why is accomplishing this important to you?

Step 2: What do you need to do in order to achieve your goal(s)? Create a list of everything you believe you need to do in order to accomplish your goal(s).

Step 3: Circle items from step 2 that are within your immediate control.

Step 4: The items you circled in step 3 become your process goals. These are the items that you have direct control over (daily habits).

*(continued on next page)*

the way they walked in told me there was some jockeying going on. It seemed to me that they were vying to be the alpha male. Not just in our throwing group but for the men's team too.

"Hi, guys," I said. "Let's get ready to warm up. I'll show you some different ways to get started in case you beat me to practice in the future."

As I led Brandon and Luis through their warm-up, I made it a point to engage in conversation about things outside track. I did a poor job of this at Fredonia, and with a fresh start, I wanted to make sure my athletes knew I cared about them as individuals.

"Did you guys have a good day at school?" I asked. "Hopefully nothing too challenging today."

"All good, Coach," replied Brandon.

"How about you, Luis? How was your day?"

"Pretty good, Coach. Can we talk after practice? I need to talk to you about something," Luis said.

"Of course. We'll have time to

talk after."

I knew something was up, but I wasn't quite sure yet. At this point, I had a bad feeling about that course Luis wanted to drop.

Our first practice went better than expected. I had an hour with both Brandon and Luis to focus on learning to turn with the weight. I was able to break down each step of the weight and hammer throw process for them in a way that I thought they easily understood. Before Jess arrived at 5:00 p.m., the guys were already taking one-turn throws with the 35-pound weight.

Jess threw the weight last year. She had a better grasp on the concept of turning with a weight than the guys did. This made sense to me. She had a background in swimming and gymnastics and was able to hit specific weight throw positions more efficiently than her muscle-bound teammates. Throughout the rest of the practice, we worked on the small pieces of weight throw throwing mechanics to ensure everyone

What sacrifices am I willing to make to achieve my goals?

What talents and skills do I need to acquire to achieve my goals?

Whom do I have to work with to accomplish my goals?

What problems am I going to have to overcome to achieve my goals?

What kinds of choices am I going to have to make (or not make) in order to achieve my goals?

would be safe and have a rewarding experience.

I could tell that Brandon and Luis were going to be good for each other. Even though Luis had never thrown before, he was going to push Brandon in practice. Which in turn was going to lead to both of them getting better, maybe not growing at the same pace but definitely moving forward in the right direction. After we wrapped up the first practice of the season, I discussed goals and the process of goal setting with Brandon, Luis, and Jess.

I gave each of them a goal-setting sheet to review, encouraging them to think about what they wanted to accomplish during the season.

"Nothing has to be written in stone," I said. "I want you to think about what you want to accomplish this season and why accomplishing that goal is important to you. When you realize the importance of attaining something meaningful to you, you will be willing to make sacrifices in order to accomplish that goal. If your Everest isn't important to you, you won't be willing to take the necessary steps to climb your mountain."

"Does anyone have any questions about that?"

"No, Coach," Brandon quickly replied. "Time to start climbing."

"Jess, you should go get some dinner. It looks like you've been going all day," I said.

"Before everyone leaves," I said, "I bought everyone a present."

"A present, on the first day?" Brandon replied.

"Let's not get carried away, friends. I brought everyone a journal. A marble notebook. This is where I want you to keep track of your training, your thoughts, your goals. Things like that. I know it's old school, but if anything, this journal will act as an accountability partner. If you skip a workout, your journal will know. If you don't track your training throws, your journal will know. I'll help you start tracking tomorrow at practice. But for now I'd like you to use the first page to write out your goals for the season. Write down what you want to accomplish this season."

"Coach, I just got out of a three-hour lab. My brain is fried. I'll see you tomorrow," Jess replied.

As Jess gathered up her gear and headed out, Brandon opened up his notebook and started writing. While he was writing, it gave Luis and I a chance to talk in private.

"Luis, did you still want to talk?"

"Yeah, Coach. So I have a meeting with my advisor tomorrow morning. I'm going to drop the science class I'm taking. I can't earn a poor grade, or I'm going to lose my scholarship," Luis said.

"OK, but are you sure your advisor has a one-credit class for you to register for?" I replied. "If you aren't registered for twelve credit hours, you will not be able to practice with us for the remainder of the semester."

For the next twenty minutes, Luis and I spoke about this science course, what it meant to be academically eligible, and the prospects of registering for the one-credit course.

"Luis, I don't want you to miss out on track this fall, because you'll fall to eleven credit hours. Is there anything you can do to make up missed work? Have you met with your professor to discuss your concerns? Can you find a tutor? We have a lot of time left this semester. You can still earn a decent grade and keep your scholarship."

"Well, I haven't gone to this class that much. She's given some quizzes when I haven't been there, so I earned a zero. It is my fault," Luis replied.

"I know I shared a lot there with you, but it's really important to try to get ahead of this in the future. Missing one or two classes is fine, but just not showing up because you don't want to isn't OK. You still have to earn at least a 2.0 GPA to be academically eligible. Make sure you give your other classes your best effort, OK?"

"I'll give you a call tomorrow and let you know," Luis said.

Despite this conversation with Luis, I thought my first practice back as a throwing coach went really well. I was able to get both Brandon and Luis taking full throws in an hour. They weren't all necessarily good throws, but they managed to get by. I felt good about myself in the sense that I hadn't officially coached in quite a few years and seemed to have made a positive impact on Luis's life by explaining the eligibility process. I never really had a serious conversation with anyone at Fredonia about their grades. I often joked about how poor my grades were, but that wasn't leading by example. I was a poor example of how a student-athlete should carry themselves. I was more focused on getting the throwers at Fredonia to throw farther. Through one practice at Nazareth, I thought I was going to be playing a different role in my athletes' lives. I also thought Jess would be the glue that kept the group together. She was much older than they were—more mature and more responsible.

## CHAPTER 19

# THE ART OF JOURNALING

I WAS ALSO HAPPY I introduced the training journals to everyone before they left. I didn't really keep a good training journal until after I graduated from Fredonia. I vaguely remember some of the more difficult weight-room training sessions with Coach Barr, but before that, I really can't recall anything of significance.

I attended a track and field coaches conference in Ohio back in November 2004. I attended Jud Logan's breakout session in which he talked about lifting and throwing volume, specifically that no two throwers are alike and should be treated as such. He then pulled out an old and faded black-and-white marble notebook. He shared with the attendees that it was one of his training journals from the winter of 2004 as he was preparing for the 2004 Olympic Trials. He also shared that he had dozens of them and referred to them as his accountability partner. He passed it around for everyone to look through. Inside, he had detailed notes describing each training session completed from January 2004 to March 2004. He listed out each throw, each lift, and how each session felt. I was surprised to see how much commentary he included with his training sessions.

While others were taking notes of his throwing session volume, I was mesmerized by the detail he included about each training session—how he felt, how he rated the session, how much sleep he got the night before, etc.

Since then, I've always given my throwers a new journal every fall. In theory, a journal should last one season. By graduation, an athlete should be able to fill four complete journals—four hundred pages of training that they can use to reflect on. I always encourage my athletes to write their goals on the very first page of their journal. I do this for a couple of reasons. Most importantly, when they open their journal, they'll be able to see their goals written down. Everything that follows on those pages should help support the achievement of those written goals. Accountability comes into play with teammates and coaches as well.

At Fredonia, I had a couple of throwers write down the goal of wanting to throw the 35-pound weight over 50' and the hammer over 165'. What followed in their journals were blank pages of nothing. They didn't keep track of their training. When we would discuss their training and progress, they didn't have anything to offer, because they didn't keep track of their training. It made it difficult for me to assist them if they weren't taking the time to write down what they were doing. I'd share this with their teammates, and then their teammates would get on them for not keeping track of training, skipping training sessions, etc. On the flip side, I've had athletes keep track of everything they've done in training—weight room and throwing. I feel that those conversations are more powerful because the athletes and I are able to figure out what else may be going on in the athlete's life that is not allowing them to achieve their goals. In these conversations, I've discussed rest, recovery, nutrition, etc. —other facets of throwing that are often overlooked, in my opinion, with DIII athletes. Even when I suggest to our athletes at Alfred State that they should try to get at least seven to eight hours of sleep a night everyone laughs and giggles. As they have heard, as well as many other of the athletes I've coached, it's difficult to accomplish your goals and achieve your aspirations on three to four hours of sleep a night with poor nutritional habits. The journal became a powerful coaching tool that I've introduced and shared with all my athletes since bringing it back from that coaching conference in November 2004.

# CHAPTER 20
# HOLD YOURSELF AND OTHERS ACCOUNTABLE

THAT NIGHT AFTER PRACTICE, I shared some thoughts with my wife. "I hope his academic advisor is being honest with him about the courses," I said to Laura. "I encouraged Luis to stay enrolled in the course, but he told me that he would lose his scholarship if he failed."

"Sometimes you need to be held accountable to your own expectations," said Laura. "He needs to be accountable for himself. The college is expecting him to maintain a certain GPA to earn his scholarship. If he doesn't do that, he needs to be held accountable for his decisions—or in this case, the lack of decision-making that led him down this path."

"I think his advisor should be held accountable as well. Why would she let him drop a course that he has to take again anyway and possibly fall ineligible? My advisor at Fredonia didn't let me drop a course. I failed it and had to take it over. They got paid twice for the same course," I said.

"The college doesn't care about Luis. The college cares that Luis is paying tuition; otherwise, they probably don't even know who he is," said Laura.

"Look at you," I said. "That sounds rather harsh, don't you think? He is a freshman; he should be given a little bit of slack."

"Should he?" Laura shot back. "Why should he be given some slack? Because he is on the track team?"

"No, not because he is on the track team but because nobody probably explained this stuff to him," I said.

Laura responded, "The NCAA or the college doesn't care about that. He should have been paying attention in the NCAA meeting he had to attend. You sat through that meeting too, remember?"

"Yeah, I remember," I said begrudgingly.

"That isn't the point. The point is that in college you, as a student, need to be held accountable for your actions. His actions, or lack thereof, led him to this point in his freshman year. He should be held accountable for his actions–in this case, not being able to compete this fall semester if he doesn't maintain the required credit hours," Laura responded.

"Yeah, I guess you are right. But I do think his advisor should be held accountable too, especially if he isn't able to register for that course," I said. "We'll see how things play out tomorrow at practice."

I received a text message from Luis early the following morning. Luis shared that he would be a little late to practice because he needed to take care of something. I didn't want to pry into what he had going on, so I told him that I was looking forward to seeing him at practice later that afternoon.

Brandon and Jess beat me to practice later that afternoon. They were already warming up when I walked into the auxiliary gymnasium.

"Hello there," I said with a smile. "How was your day at school?"

"Pretty good, Coach. My lab was a little rough, but I'm happy to be here at practice," Jess said, smiling.

"Coach, I had a good day too. My Italian class is going really well. I got a ninety-seven on my midterm," said Brandon.

"Sounds like you two have had a pretty good day," I remarked. "Hopefully, this is the easiest, most stress-free part of your day."

"I have lots of studying to do tonight, Coach," Jess shot back. "These PT courses are getting more difficult."

"Well, I mean, you did pass Human Anatomy I and II. I think you are in pretty good shape," I said.

I had Brandon and Jess pick up where we left off the previous day. We started our training session with more learn-to-turn drills. I followed that with release drills with a medicine ball, progressed to releases with a weight, to one-wind and one-turn releases with the weight. Jess had a knack for the weight. We added an additional turn, making her progression a one-wind and two-turn throw.

Luis arrived midway through practice. From what I could tell, Luis had a dejected look on his face. He didn't look happy at all.

"Hi, Luis," I said. "Take a few minutes and get ready. You can join us after you warm up."

Luis started warming up while I was working with Brandon and Jess. After a few more throws with the weight, I told Brandon and Jess to get some water and take a break for a minute.

# CHAPTER 21
# IT'S OVER BEFORE IT EVEN STARTED

"HOW WAS YOUR MEETING WITH YOUR ACADEMIC ADVISOR?" I asked Luis as he started getting ready for practice.

"Not good, Coach," remarked Luis. "I had my meeting with my academic advisor. I dropped my science class."

"OK, that's what you wanted, right?" I asked.

"Yeah, Coach, but I wasn't able to register for that one-credit course. It filled up before my meeting this morning."

I'm not good at hiding my emotions. Luis could tell I was disappointed.

"I'm really sorry, Coach," Luis said with a nervous look on his face. "I messed up. I'm really sorry."

"You don't have to be sorry about anything, Luis. I'm not mad at you. I'm actually disappointed in your advisor. How did she let this happen?"

"I don't know, Coach. She told me that I would be able to register for the class. When we tried online, we couldn't. The class filled up."

"Luis, it's OK. The unfortunate thing is that you aren't allowed to practice with us for the rest of the semester. You won't be able to compete either. Your fall semester is done. Done before it really started."

Luis and I continued our conversation for a few more minutes before Luis gathered his gear and left the practice facility. Brandon and Jess took a few more throws before calling it for the day. I told them that Luis would not be with us the remainder of the semester because of academic ineligibility.

I shared a similar message with James.

"Well, I'm not sure if I'll ever see Luis again," I said to James. "After one practice, I'm not sure he'll come back. He really doesn't have a reason to. I'll continue to share workouts with him, and hopefully he comes back and joins us in January."

James didn't seem as bothered by this as I was. He had much more coaching experience than me and was probably used to situations like this happening. In my short coaching career, this was the first time I had an athlete drop under the required number of credits and fall ineligible to compete. I was upset with myself. I'm not sure if I had reason to be, but I felt like it was my responsibility, and I had let Luis down.

Luis's first semester as a track and field athlete ended before it started. Luis attended one practice before falling below the minimum twelve-credit-hour requirement overseen by the NCAA. Luis was now registered for eleven credit hours. As I watched Luis walk out of the training facility that Wednesday evening, I thought it would be the last time I would ever see him.

That evening I sent Luis an email. I encouraged him to continue training through November and December to be ready to rejoin the team in January. I also wrote to Luis that while he was training without the team that if he decided to return to the team in January, he should have a couple of specific goals outlined. I wrote:

*Dear Luis,*

*I'm glad we were able to speak this afternoon at practice. I understand that making the transition to college is a difficult one. It took me a couple of semesters at Fredonia to get my act together.*

*I encourage you to take the time over the next couple of months to continue to train. Although you cannot train with your teammates, you should still complete the workouts to better prepare yourself to make a successful return in January. Before you come back to the team, I want you to think about a couple of things. First, I want you to think about a goal or two that you would want to accomplish this season. I know you've never thrown the weight or hammer before, but here are some links to other collegiate throwers. Watch what they do and think about what you would want to accomplish. You can include some distances, if that makes it easier for you. I also want you to think about why you want to accomplish these goals. Why are they important to you? What type of satisfaction would it bring you to say you were able to accomplish what you said you wanted to accomplish?*

*Please stay in touch over the next couple of months. I'm here for you if you need anything. Don't hesitate to call or text.*

*Your Coach,*
*Coach Infurna*

I sent this email at 10:30 p.m.

"Laura, I just sent Luis an email with ideas to think about over the next couple of months with things I encouraged him to focus on."

"Do you think he'll do what you asked?" Laura said.

"I'm not sure. We didn't really have the time to develop a strong relationship. We only had one practice together. I don't think that's enough to keep him on the team. I'm not sure he'll come back in January."

"Stay in constant contact," Laura said encouragingly. "Let him know you are thinking about him. Ask him how he is doing, or if he needs help with anything."

# CHAPTER 22
# CAN YOU BE LED FROM AFAR?

TRAINING LEADING UP TO NOVEMBER break was going really well. Brandon and Jess had found a stride together; they pushed each other in the weight room and with throwing. They worked really well together. I shared as such on multiple occasions in practice. My only concern was that they very rarely mentioned anything about Luis. When I asked about him, Brandon would share that he would see him in the weight room and that they didn't hang out as much socially.

To a certain extent, this bothered me. Brandon and Jess were under no obligation to include Luis in team-related activities, but it seemed that they had shut him out. But I also remember thinking to myself that Luis wasn't technically a member of the team anymore, at least for the time being.

I stayed in constant contact with Luis through November. I'd ask for updates about training, how his other classes were going, and if there was anything I could do to help him through the rest of the semester. Most of his replies were short and to the point. Usually that he was OK or that his grades were fine or that training was going really well. Nothing of substance. I didn't have a good feeling about him coming back in January.

What I didn't realize at the time was that I was making a positive impact on his life. This came to light one day in school. At the time, I was working for the Center for Youth in Rochester. I was assigned to a Rochester City School District elementary school, and one day, during some downtime in my schedule, a gentleman walked into my classroom with another school resource officer and introduced himself as Mr. Rivera, Luis's dad. What I didn't know at the time was that Luis's dad worked for the Rochester City School District as a traveling school resource officer. He made it a point on this November day to visit my building, introduce himself to me, and ask me how Luis's semester was going.

"Are you Charles?" asked Mr. Rivera.

"Um, yes, I am. How can I help you, Mr. Rivera?"

"How is Luis doing in school?"

"I think Luis is doing pretty well. Have you had the chance to talk to him about the semester?"

"He doesn't share much with me, but he has talked a lot about you," Mr. Rivera said.

"Really? Well, don't believe everything he's told you," I remember saying, half-jokingly, not knowing what exactly Luis has shared with his dad.

"Luis told me what you did last month. You know, with the credits."

"Mr. Rivera, I'm really sorry about that," Charles said. "I'm sorry he isn't able to train with us this semester. Like Luis, I thought his advisor had everything squared away."

"Luis told me that you encouraged him to stay in the course and try his best. That you told him that you would have helped him with a tutor on campus and that he should be accountable for what happened."

I wasn't sure what direction this conversation was going. I didn't know if Mr. Rivera was mad at me or happy with what I had shared with Luis.

"Mr. Rivera, I'm really sorry. I really wanted Luis to stay enrolled and try to get his grades up. Now he'll have to take another science class at some point in his college career. He really didn't do himself any favors by dropping the course."

"I know he didn't. I want to say thank you for helping him," Mr. Rivera said.

"Thank you?" I said. "I didn't really do much to help him. If anything, his GPA might have been worse if he stayed in the class."

"Luis told me that you had a talk about accountability," Mr. Rivera said sternly. "What did you talk to him about?"

"I told Luis that since he is enrolled in college now, he needs to hold himself more accountable for his actions. I also told him that he is the only person that is going to determine whether he graduates on time. Yes, we have a support system at college, but ultimately he has to do the work required of him."

Mr. Rivera continued looking intently at me as I continued to discuss the last in-person conversation I had with Luis.

"You see, Mr. Rivera, track and field is an amazing sport. I believe you get out of it what you put in. If you work hard, set goals, and prioritize what you need to be accountable for, you'll be successful," I said. "I want Luis to excel, but his grades are more important. That is my top priority: to ensure he meets academic standards that will allow him to compete and graduate on time."

As the bell for the next period rang, Mr. Rivera said, "Charles, whatever you do, please take care of my boy. We haven't always been on the same page, but it sounds like he trusts you. Make sure you take care of him when he comes back next semester."

*Take care of my boy*, I thought to myself. *This did not go like I thought it would. He wants me to take care of his son, but I've already failed him.*

Later that night, I recounted my conversation with Mr. Rivera to Laura.

"Guess who I spoke to today in school?" I asked Laura as we sat down for dinner.

"Who?" Laura replied.

"Mr. Rivera, Luis's dad."

"What did he have to say?"

"Well, at first I thought he was upset with me."

"Upset with you? Why would he be upset with you?"

"I guess he and Luis had a conversation about what I told Luis last month. Luis told his dad about our accountability conversation."

"And?" Laura asked anxiously.

"He told me to take care of his son. Mr. Rivera told me to continue working with Luis and to make sure he does what he needs to do in order to graduate on time."

"Really?"

"Yeah, he told me to take care of Luis. I thought the conversation was going to go in a different direction, but it didn't. He wants me to take care of him and make sure he has a good experience with our team."

"That sounds great. Good thing you've continued to stay in constant communication with Luis. That lets him know that you care about him."

"How does Luis know I care about him?"

"He knows because you've kept at it. You text him every day, and he texts back. If you didn't care, you wouldn't do it," Laura said. "You are showing him that he means more to you than just being another thrower on the team. He hasn't thrown yet, and you speak to him more than anyone else I know."

"I probably send him quite a few text messages a day. I just want to make sure he graduates on time."

"I feel like schools need to do more for their students once they are on campus. I don't want Luis to fall into the same trap the others fell into at Fredonia. The same trap I almost fell into. You know, they start and then disappear before you realize it," I said. "There needs to be a better support system in place. Not just for athletes but all students. Students on campus need someone to guide them. Like a light. Keeping a path lit for them. The right path that's going to get them where they want to go. A light that gives them what they need—guidance. They need a lightgiver."

For context, I did not create the term *lightgiver*. I watched a presentation that Jud Logan gave, and he talked about a lightgiver in his life. Someone who illuminated a path for him brighter than he could illuminate for himself. That term stuck with me. I've used that term a lot, and the credit all goes to Jud Logan.

"A lightgiver?" Laura said.

"Yes, a lightgiver. Someone who will illuminate a path brighter for them than they can illuminate for themselves. A beacon of light keeping them on the right path, making sure they don't stray away from their goals. A light that holds them accountable. A light that allows them to far exceed their expectations of themselves!"

"How can you be their lightgiver?" Laura asked. "What do you think you should do differently from what you did at Fredonia? You held your state athletes accountable. None of your athletes failed out or had to change majors because of not meeting academic standards.

What do you think was missing?"

"I think I should hold their hands."

"Hold their hands?" Laura asked.

"Yeah, I should hold their hands more. I think that's what they need. Not just freshmen athletes but all the athletes on our team. They need to know there are people on campus who care about them. Everyone can use a lightgiver, someone who will illuminate a path for you. When you lose your path, your lightgiver will continue to illuminate their path. Unconditional support."

# CHAPTER 23
# WHERE DO YOU WANT TO GO?

THIS CONVERSATION WITH MY WIFE stuck with me for a few reasons. First, it was the first time I had shared with someone what I really thought about the collegiate system as far as accepting students who the colleges may have known would struggle and possibly fail out. Second, it was the first time I shared in great detail what happened to me at Fredonia. My whole life trajectory changed when I made the switch from secondary to elementary education. Maybe in the moment not a big deal, but a huge decision in the greater scheme of things. I was nineteen years old, earned a B- in a class called Doing History 201, and was encouraged by my advisor to switch to elementary education rather than retake the course another semester. I didn't expect her—my advisor—to give me a B unless I earned it, but she could have at least had a more detailed conversation with me about the ramifications of this decision. I didn't have to get permission from my parents or anything. One day I'm thinking I'm going to be a high school social studies teacher, and the next day I'm enrolling in math for elementary educators. If Dr. Litwicki, my advisor and chair of the history department at the time, had encouraged me to stay in secondary education because she believed in me, I know I would have put more effort into my coursework. That wasn't the case. She just passed me on to another department. I was going to try my best to ensure that didn't happen to Luis either.

Our fall semester was quickly coming to a close. Brandon, Jess, and I had been practicing three times a week since the end of October. I tried my best to ensure that we followed a similar practice agenda each time we met. During these training sessions, I encouraged Jess and Brandon to think about what felt good about their throws, and to try to replicate those "feels" with each successive throw. I also preached to them that they should develop consistent routines that would help them feel more comfortable in practice and in competition.

Two days after the Cornell meet, I asked Luis to meet me for coffee on campus. We met, had a great conversation about his grades, the courses he registered for that upcoming spring semester, and what his expectations were for the spring.

"Do you still have the notebook I gave you?" I asked.

"Of course I do," Luis responded.

Luis took out his journal and shared it with me. I flipped through page after page of detailed notes documenting Luis's weight-room training for that fall semester.

"Luis, this is amazing!" I shared. "This is very detailed. I'm impressed with the work ethic you've demonstrated this fall semester."

"Thank you, Coach. You really lit a fire under me at our first practice. That was the first time I felt as though a coach really cared about me."

"Luis, I appreciate you sharing that. I think you are moving forward in the right direction," I said.

"Moving in the right direction, Coach? What does that mean?" Luis asked.

"It means you did everything you were supposed to do, but there is a little bit more, Luis."

"What else is left, Coach?"

"Well, from the look of your journal, you definitely held yourself accountable this semester. I think you held yourself to a higher standard. But I think there is more. You have something about you, the way you carry yourself, that tells me you are willing to do what it takes to achieve your goals. It's like a look. Some athletes have it. Like a little twinkle in their eyes. What you did is the hard part. Teaching you how to throw is easy. You have the want to. Now we have to figure out the know-how."

"What do you think you want to do this spring?" I asked excitedly. "What types of goals do you have for yourself?"

"I want to break the school records, Coach. I want to throw at our indoor and outdoor conference meets."

I almost chuckled when I heard Luis share that aloud. Not that he wanted to break our school records but the distances. The Nazareth College track and field program was still in its infancy—maybe two or three years old. Our throwing records were not very good. I didn't feel comfortable sharing that with Luis—yet. I knew he would realize they weren't really formidable goals once he attended his first indoor meet of the spring semester.

"To be honest, Luis," I started, "I think you should set your sights much higher than breaking our school records. Being a school record holder is nice, but those marks might not qualify you for the conference championship meets."

"Really?" Luis said dejectedly. "I thought that breaking the school records would be a good thing."

"Oh, breaking the school records would be great, but I think you can set your sights much higher. I think you can have two standout seasons as a freshman—both indoor and outdoor. I think qualifying for the state meet would be something you should aim for."

As Luis and I were having this conversation, I checked the qualifying marks for the indoor and outdoor state meets.

"This is how far you would need to throw in order to qualify, Luis," I shared.

"Coach, those numbers are big! I'd have to throw really far to qualify for indoor and outdoor states. Do you think I can do it?"

"Luis, I know you've never thrown in a track and field meet before, but I believe you have the opportunity to set this conference on fire. You trained all fall when you didn't have to. That's better than most of the other athletes on campus, and probably most athletes we will be competing against this year," I said with a heightened sense of excitement.

"You really think so?" Luis said with a sense of trepidation in his voice.

We continued our conversation for a few more minutes—what the training schedule would look like this spring semester, weight-room training sessions, our schedule, etc.

"You'll be living like a rock star, Luis," I said. "For the first week back on campus, all you'll be responsible for is throwing and training. You don't have to worry about classes for almost two weeks."

"What will our practice schedule look like?" Luis asked.

"Well, I'll still be in school, so we won't start practice until our normal time. In the morning, you'll have your weight-room session or a swim session with the rest of the team. You'll then have pretty much all morning and early afternoon to yourself before we throw."

"And that's it? That's all we'll be doing?"

"Yes, it's a pretty low-key week, but very important. You'll basically be throwing in your first meet after five consecutive practice days. Not what I'd usually like, but I think you'll be fine."

Before I left, I gave Luis a goal-setting activity sheet.

"Before you come back in a few weeks, I'd like you to complete this sheet for me. It'll help me chart a smooth course for you."

"A smooth course? Where are we going, Coach?" Luis chuckled.

"That depends on where *you* want to go, my friend. You see, it's my job to get you where you want to go. If you want to throw at states, we both know you'll need to hit a certain number or be ranked in the top twenty-four. Completing this sheet honestly will help me get you where you want to go. It'll be more difficult if we don't have a direction."

I continued, "If you want to just be another athlete on the team, you don't need to complete this. You can have fun, travel with the team on the weekends, and not be expected to contribute."

"I want to do more than contribute, Coach," Luis said while staring intently into my eyes.

"I know you do, Luis. This sheet will help you stay accountable to your expectations. If you expect to throw at states, well, then you'll need to follow the steps. If you just want to throw, well, then you don't need to waste your time. Just show up and don't think anything about it. But I think I already know you better than that. I know you want to be great. This will help you get there faster with fewer detours along the way."

We continued to discuss Luis's goals for the season and what he wanted to accomplish during this freshman year. I knew Luis was special. He was different from other athletes I've coached in the past. It really is difficult to put my finger on it, but he had that "it" factor. Similar to when someone of stature walks into a room and everyone turns to see who it is–Luis had that aura about him. The way he was looking at me, I knew he was going to do what he said. I didn't know much about his background yet, but I could tell that the chip on his shoulder was due to something from his past. After spending a decade working with students in schools, you tend to hone in on things like that. He was harboring something, carrying something with him. I didn't know what it was, but I knew it wouldn't take long to find out.

"Luis, when I talk about expectations, I'm referring to what you ultimately think you can achieve. You see, everyone has this Mount Everest they are climbing."

"Now we are climbing mountains, Coach?" Luis said with a chuckle.

"Well, sort of. You see, everyone is chasing something. You shared you wanted to break our school records. That's great, but breaking those records won't get you qualified for big meets. Once you break the weight or hammer record, then what?"

"Then I'll keep breaking records," Luis said confidently.

"I know you'll continue breaking records. I just think you should have higher expectations and aspirations for yourself. What I'd like you to do in the next page of your journal is write down your aspirations. Take what you write down on this worksheet and then write them down in your journal."

"I can do that, Coach. I'll write down what I want to accomplish this season and throughout my throwing career."

"And one more thing, Luis. Question one is the most important: Why is achieving these goals important to you? Whatever you write down, really think about why you want to achieve these goals."

"Sure, Coach. I can write that down," Luis replied.

"Luis, I think this is enough for today. I don't want to take too much time away from your study time. Please take the time to complete this activity sheet. You'll set the destination, and I'll chart the course for us. I think you'll surprise yourself this season. If you are able to answer the first question honestly, you'll achieve whatever you want!"

# CHAPTER 24
# EXPECTATIONS AND ACCOUNTABILITY

LUIS DID INDEED RETURN TO THE COLLEGE TRACK AND FIELD TEAM in January 2013. He returned in very good shape and was ready to start his collegiate track and field career. Before the first practice started, I shared some thoughts with Brandon, Jess, and Luis.

"Welcome back, everyone. I'm happy to see you here! I know you all worked hard over break. You can definitely tell you took the five weeks off seriously and that you completed your weight-room workouts. Did you all complete your goal-setting activity sheets?"

"Here is mine, Coach," said Brandon.

"I got ya, Coach," said Jess.

While Jess and Brandon started warming up, Luis approached me.

"Here are my goals, Coach," Luis said intently.

"Thanks, Luis. Wow, you really spent a lot of time working on this. I'm really impressed," I said excitedly. "Tell me about your 'why'?"

Luis started, "I want to be successful, Coach. I want to throw far to show others that you don't need to throw in high school to set high expectations for yourself. I want to learn how to become a great collegiate thrower."

"That's great, Luis," I shared. "I'm glad you want to learn. Throwing is all about learning. You'll learn a lot about yourself in the circle. Sometimes it's a humbling experience, and sometimes it's an exhilarating one. Sometimes both feelings in the same meet. Sometimes with the same throw," Charles chuckled to himself.

I sat at my desk reviewing my coaching journal the night before our first indoor meet of the spring semester. I remember thinking to myself that I thought everyone was ready to compete. They worked hard those first few weeks of the semester. They deserved to have at least one bright spot in the competition. Something that they could latch on to that keeps them coming back. I'm not sure if it's a good analogy or not, but it's something I've shared with all the athletes I've coached. It's always important to find at least one bright spot in every competition–that is what keeps you coming back. Like in golf, you may have a bogey or double bogey every hole, but that one birdie keeps you coming back!

"What are you doing?" Laura asked. "You're up late and have to get up early tomorrow morning. Don't miss the bus."

"Don't miss the bus. Please don't remind me," I said. "I've had enough missed-bus situations occur for a lifetime," I said with a smile. "But I'm a little nervous. I think I prepared everyone for the meet as best I could."

"It's only been five practice sessions. I wouldn't expect much from anyone this first meet. You know how they go."

"Yeah, I know," I said. "I'm not worried about distances. I just hope they are ready to compete. You know, don't get nervous competing at a Division I meet."

"You've talked about expectations and all those things. I'm sure everyone will be fine tomorrow."

"I think everyone will. I sent everyone a message earlier tonight. I told them they are ready to compete and stick to their routines and rituals."

"You and your routines and rituals," Laura laughed.

"It's important to have those things in place. It helps create a sense of consistency and calmness. Doing the same thing every day in practice and then replicating that process in the heat of the moment."

"Yeah, yeah. You've shared all of this before," Laura retorted. "It's more than that, right? All the stuff you shared with me about Coach Barr. They aren't going to throw well if they don't take care of themselves outside practice."

"That's what I'm concerned with. I remember how I acted as a freshman."

"You still act like that," Laura said with a smile.

"I know, but I'm not competing anymore. I'm trying to help them. I just hope I haven't pushed them too much too soon. Our first meet went well. I want to make sure we keep the momentum going."

"Then don't set high expectations for yourself. If they throw well, that's great. If not, no big deal. It isn't your career at stake here. You are a volunteer coach, emphasis on the *volunteer*. I'm sure the throwers are happy to have you around. Not like where we came from," Laura said. "You better get to bed soon. You don't want to miss the bus for the first meet."

## CHAPTER 25

# IT COULD HAVE GONE MUCH WORSE

Luis's first meet of his collegiate career came on January 18, 2013. In all honesty, it was a miracle that Luis actually competed at this meet. I wasn't a fan of competing after only having learned the event a few days prior, but what better way to learn to compete than by competing?

The meet was low-key by early-season standards. We were competing at SUNY Brockport. They had recently opened a brand-new indoor facility. It would turn into a facility Luis and I would enjoy traveling to and competing at. On this day, it was a test to see how well Luis would handle the atmosphere of collegiate competition.

"How are you feeling today?" I asked. "Ready for your first meet?"

"Of course, Coach! I'm ready," replied Luis.

In his first competition of his collegiate career, Luis threw the 35-pound weight a modest 34'2". He finished in ninth place overall, barely making the finals. In his first meet, Luis was able to squeak in a decent opening performance and make the finals of his first weight throw competition. He managed to catch something else as well.

"Coach, this is an incredible feeling! I can't believe it. I made the finals!" Luis exclaimed excitedly.

"Yes, you did. In fact, you came really close to breaking our school record," I said.

"Really?"

"Yes, really. Do you remember the conversation we had a couple of months ago about expectations?"

"Yeah, I remember."

"Expectations are important, Luis. They, along with how we hold ourselves accountable, guide us along our journey. You took the first step toward climbing your Everest today. It is a step in the right direction."

"I still have a lot of work to do, don't I?" Luis said.

"Every day and every practice is an opportunity to grow as a thrower and an individual. I think you've been bit by the competitive bug."

"The competitive bug?" Luis asked, puzzled.

"Yes, the competitive bug. It's like a metaphor for wanting to continue to compete and improve yourself. To get better at something. To not settle for just being OK, but to really want to continue improving. In track, and especially with throwing, it's really easy to see who wins and loses. I have a feeling you won't just be making the finals but scoring at some point during this season."

"You really think so?"

"I absolutely do. You competed in your first meet after six training sessions and qualified for the finals. You beat a lot of good throwers today. I wouldn't tell you I think you could be good someday if I didn't believe it!"

I could tell Luis was excited about competing in his first meet.

He was very social, engaged in conversation with many of the other throwers and athletes around him, but also paid attention to the other competitors he was throwing against. The winning throw was 45'2". Nothing to write home about. I knew it. Luis knew it too.

"Coach," Luis started, "I'll beat these guys someday."

"I know you will. Probably sooner than you think you will. Much sooner."

As we drove back to Nazareth from Brockport, all I could think about was the conversation Luis and I had as we were packing up and getting ready to head out. Luis realized that after a few training sessions he could compete at the Division III level. Nobody knew he didn't throw all fall semester. And here he was in the finals at SUNY Brockport.

There was something about watching Luis compete that was a good indicator of his future success. He paid attention to what was going on around him, but he didn't let it bother him. He was excited to compete, but it didn't seem overwhelming to him. He was able to remain calm and entered the circle the same way every throw. I didn't want to give him too many cues or adjustments to make. I repeatedly told him to pick one thing to focus on—smoother wind, weight placement in level with his nose, or keeping his shoulders relaxed. I didn't have to tell him much. It was good to just get him out there.

## CHAPTER 26

# NOBODY CARES WHAT YOU LOOK LIKE, ONLY HOW FAR YOU THROW

To this day, I still think it is odd that our conference championship meet was held the last weekend of January. We had a solid three weeks of training coming off our holiday break. Our training sessions were as concise and efficient as possible. The one nice thing about having such an important meet so early in the season was that our athletes didn't have to worry about a huge course load building up, or the concern of having to study for midterm exams while gone for a Saturday afternoon. The meet was held at Ithaca College. Another new venue I had yet to step foot in due to my absence from coaching. The two-hour drive went by rather quickly. We left early in the morning, and most of the athletes slept on the way to the meet. A couple of athletes didn't. One of whom was Luis.

Just before we got off the Auburn, New York, exit to make the final push into Ithaca, I got up and walked to the back of the bus. By this time in the season, both Brandon and Luis had taken somewhat of a leadership role on the team. We didn't have a lot of upperclassmen, but the ones we did have didn't mind letting Luis and Brandon take the lead.

"What are you listening to?" I asked Luis.

"Coach, you don't wanna know," Luis said with a laugh. "It's too early in the morning."

"I'm surprised you aren't napping like everyone else," I said.

"Coach, I'm not like everyone else," Luis replied confidently.

"Well, it sounds like whatever you are listening to is getting you ready to compete. Enjoy the last hour."

When we arrived at the facility, our throwers immediately went over to the weigh-in station to weigh in our implements. At championship meets, throwers must certify their implements, meaning they meet official guidelines. All our implements passed certification.

After everyone put their gear down, I pulled Luis aside.

"Hey, Luis," I said. "I'd like to talk to you for a second. Let's take a walk."

I brought Luis into the infield of the facility to ensure nobody else would be able to listen to our conversation.

"I want to tell you how proud I am of you. You've come a long way these past couple of weeks. You are starting to figure out this weight throw stuff, and I think you should look forward to having a nice day. Reward yourself with a great performance today. It's championship meet time. Different from Brockport."

"What do you mean by different?"

"Competing at conference championship meets is different from any other meet. Like I shared this week in practice, everyone starts today with a clean slate. Anything can happen. The best or top-seeded throwers don't always throw well in these meets. Something crazy always happens. As long as we stick to the plan we discussed earlier in the week, I think you'll surprise a lot of people today."

"OK," Luis said with a puzzled look on his face.

"I know we talked about it earlier, but I just wanted to mention again that it isn't as important to set a personal best at a meet like this. Trying to make the finals and putting yourself in position to score and make the podium is what conference meets are about."

"I got that, Coach. We talked about it on Thursday," Luis replied.

"I know. I just wanted to share that with you again. You are in great shape to have an awesome performance today. I want you to keep an even perspective on things. I know you'll be great!"

Luis had a subpar start to the competition, sitting in last place after the first round with a throw of around 28'. He picked things up in round two by setting a personal best of 36'9.5". Luis didn't improve in round three, but he had secured a position in the finals. Brandon also qualified for the finals.

"Luis, you look good today," I said.

"No, I don't, Coach. Brandon is beating me," replied Luis.

"That's OK. Healthy competition. But to be fair, both of your techniques are off today."

"That's what I'm worried about. My feet look horrible today," Luis shared with a concerned look on his face.

"OK, let's drop down in turns and try something new. You are already in seventh place. You aren't going to finish lower than that. Let's get a little more amped up before the finals start."

"Are you sure?" Luis asked.

I got a little closer to Luis so that nobody around us could hear what I was going to share.

"Luis, nobody cares what you look like in the circle. They only ask how far you threw, not how it looked."

Luis sat in seventh place going into the finals. Brandon was in sixth place. I knew for sure that one of the two was going to score Nazareth College's first men's weight throw conference championship point. It didn't matter that much to me at the time. It certainly mattered to Luis. Much more than it mattered to Brandon.

Due to the nature of this specific competition, only the top six athletes would score points for their team in this fashion—ten points for first place, eight points for second place, six points for third, four points for fourth, two points for fifth, and one point for sixth. For context, the winning 35-pound weight throw mark of the day was

Neither Brandon nor Luis improved their preliminary marks in the final three rounds of the competition. Their marks didn't improve, but their competitive nature was firmly planted that day at Ithaca College.

I noticed something about Brandon and Luis that I didn't notice before. They were friendly and cordial on campus and had been at other competitions, but this afternoon it was as though they weren't competing for the same college.

After the competition, I congratulated both Brandon and Luis for their efforts in their first conference championship. Brandon was ecstatic. Luis was beside himself.

"I should have been able to catch him [Brandon]," Luis said. "I did horrible today."

"You qualified for the finals in your first conference championship meet, and you hit a personal best. I'd call that a good day," I replied.

"That's easy for you to say. You weren't in there competing."

"Sure I was. I wasn't physically in the circle with you, but I was in here." I pointed to my heart.

"What is that supposed to mean, Coach?"

"It means that when you guys compete, I compete too. I don't feel the physical toll. I feel the emotional toll. The good and the bad. I feel all the throws," I said with a smile. "It's my job."

"I don't get it."

"Luis, I take all the throws you take. And Brandon. And Jess. I feel them all. I know what it's like to have a good day and not have it be enough. I get it. I've learned to work with it. I've taken more emotional throws than you have. I understand that you are disappointed right now. I know you set a personal best and still didn't score points for our team. It happens sometimes. It just happened to you sooner than I thought it would. This was your first conference meet. With a semester less of practice time than everyone here. I think you competed pretty well for yourself."

"Thank you, Coach. But I'm still mad I didn't catch Brandon."

"You can catch him at the next meet."

# CHAPTER 27
# BE AGGRESSIVE OR PLAY IT SAFE

DESPITE MISSING A SEMESTER OF TRAINING TIME, Luis had a fairly successful start to his collegiate indoor track and field career. He finished the season with a personal-best throw of 41'1.5" with the 35-pound weight on February 15, 2013, at the Rochester Institute of Technology. The following weekend (February 22–23) we competed at the New York State Championships (all private and public Division III colleges and universities in New York) held at St. Lawrence University. Up until competing at RIT, Luis had an up-and-down season. He would throw well one week, then follow up with a poor performance (for his standards), then throw well again. We hadn't put two solid weekends together yet, and I didn't think we would start here.

All my coaching—conversations, hype, ease, calmness—was not enough at St. Lawrence. Luis was seeded in the first flight of two and did not throw well. It was his worst performance of the season. He fouled out of the competition, which means he didn't have a fair mark of his three preliminary throws. At the time, it was difficult for the both of us. He had been training well in practice, didn't miss any weight-room sessions, and was beginning to figure out what it meant to compete.

"Coach, I'm sorry we drove all this way for nothing," Luis said after the competition. "I'm sorry. I'm embarrassed."

"Luis, there is nothing to feel bad about," I started. "Meets like this happen. Unfortunately, you got it out of your system when you were starting to really tighten up your technique. It's OK."

"It is not OK," Luis quickly retorted. "This is not how my indoor season should have ended."

"Well, let's say you would have set a personal best. Would you have been happier finishing twentieth?"

I could tell I struck a chord with that last remark.

"What's that supposed to mean, Coach?"

"It means a couple of things. You entered the circle with no fear. We talked about it earlier in the week. We knew it would have taken a throw in the 50' to make the finals. If we aren't trying to make the finals each meet, what are we working toward?" I said.

Luis looked at me intently.

"You see, you competed with no fear today. That's a difficult skill to coach someone. You weren't worried about the consequences. So you fouled out. Nobody cares. Most played it safe. You didn't. Our result wasn't what we wanted, and that is OK. You certainly didn't leave any doubt either."

"Coach, I should have made the finals."

"Luis, be honest: Do you think you could have gone over 50' today? Don't answer that yet. Think about it. I don't think we had any training throws over 44' this week. That would have put you at sixteenth. That's OK too. But we need to start thinking bigger."

Luis Rivera ready to get to work at the 2016 Division III Indoor Nationals.

Peak performance. Luis on top of the podium at the Division III Indoor Nationals.

Here, I was the first to congratulate Luis on his national title.

2016 Division III Outdoor Nationals

## 2016 Division III Outdoor Nationals

Luis showing his NCAA Outdoor championship hardware.

Dad time with Luis.

Me with my most important athletes, then . . .

. . . and now.

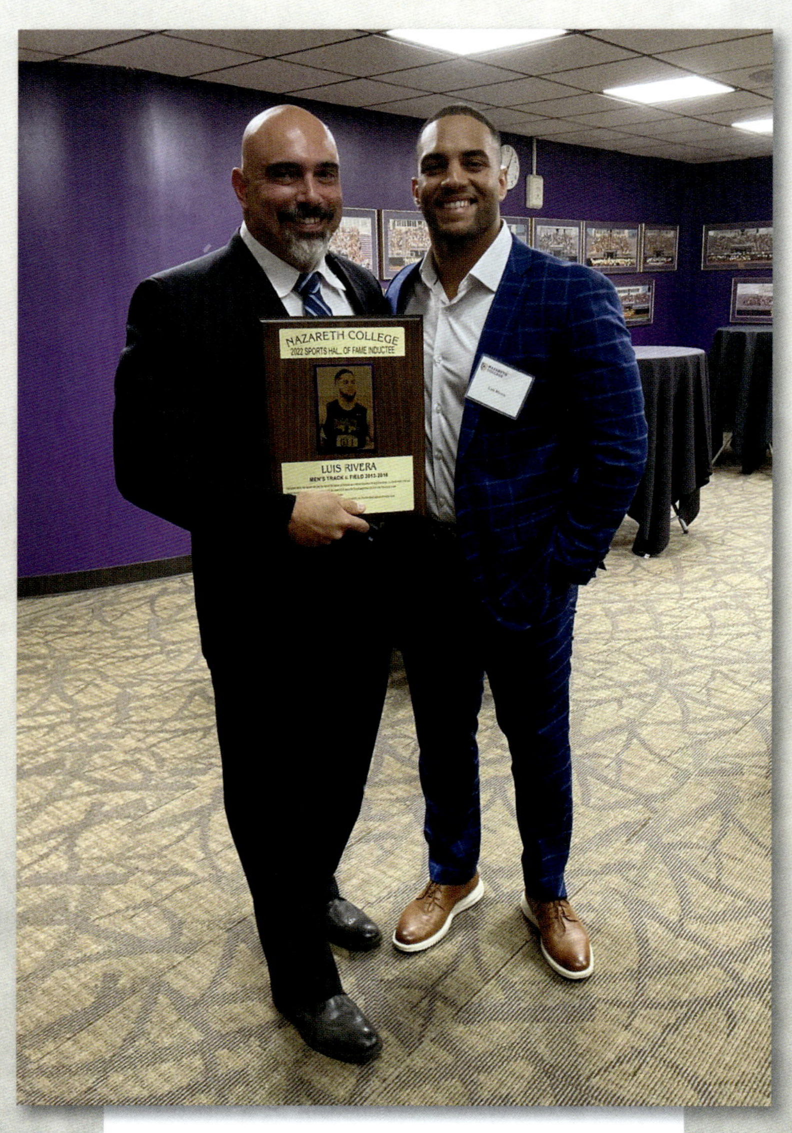


Celebrating with Luis on his induction into the Nazareth Hall of Fame.

Luis on his big night.

Luis and me before the Division III Outdoor Nationals in 2016.

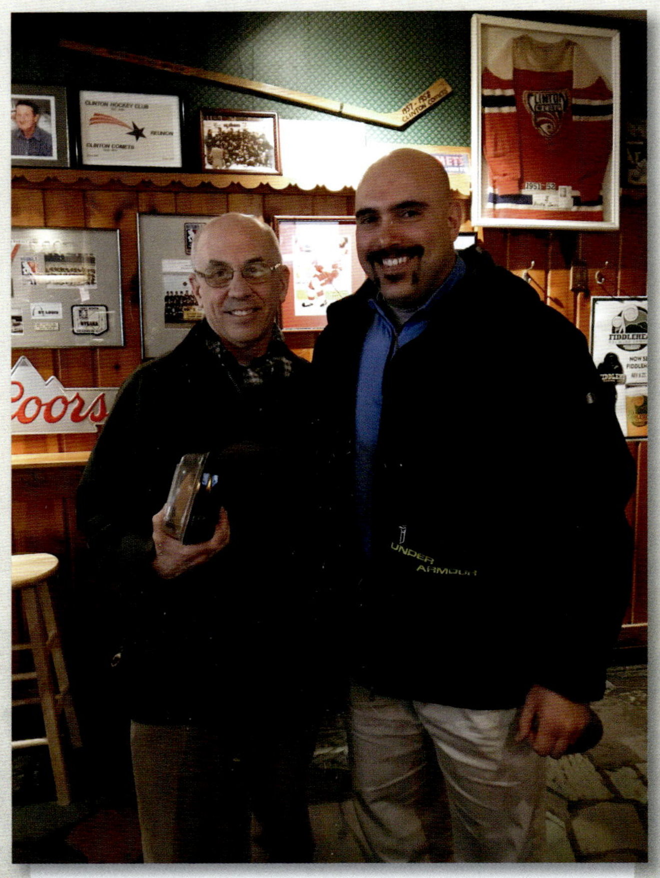


I was honored to meet with one of my coaching mentors, Dan Chambliss, in April 2018.

# CHAPTER 28
# BECOMING A BETTER COACH

BEFORE THE START OF THE OUTDOOR SEASON, I scheduled one-on-one meetings with each thrower on the team. I did this at Fredonia as a way to center the athlete and make a clean transition into the outdoor season. I asked each athlete how they thought their indoor season went—strengths, highlights, lowlights, and things they wanted to focus on during the outdoor season. I scheduled my last meeting with Luis a few days before the start of the outdoor season. We met at the main dining hall on campus.

"Hi, Luis!" I exclaimed. "Thanks for meeting me for lunch. I've never eaten at this dining hall. What would you recommend?"

"I'm not sure you want to eat anything here," Luis said with a chuckle. "The food is OK. I'd recommend the bacon cheeseburger."

"Perfect, the bacon cheeseburger and fries it is."

We found a small table by the corner to eat lunch and discuss the indoor season.

"So, what did you think of your first competitive track and field season?"

"I think it went really well. I accomplished one of my goals, but

I didn't accomplish all of them."

"Did you bring your journal with you?"

"I sure did," Luis replied.

Before looking back at Luis's original goals, I couldn't help but look through all the detailed notes Luis had taken throughout the indoor season. Meet after meet of thoughts and ideas. One caught my attention, dated February 23, 2013. Next to St. Lawrence, I could faintly make out the words *never again*.

"What does *never again* mean, Luis?" I asked.

"It means I'm never not going to make the finals of a conference championship ever again. I'm going to score at every upcoming indoor and outdoor conference meet I compete at. I'm making all the finals."

I'm sure Luis was convinced he was indeed going to make the finals of every conference championship. Even with never having thrown a 16-pound hammer before, he was confident in his abilities.

"Let's take a look at what you wrote down back in January. You said you were going to break the school records in the weight throw, hammer throw, and discus throw. Well, you accomplished one item on that list. How does that make you feel?"

"Yeah, now I realize it really wasn't going to be hard to do. I think I threw over that school record weight throw distance close to twelve times this season."

"After we first met, I had a pretty strong suspicion you were going to break that weight throw record."

"You thought so, huh?"

"I did. When I was dating Laura, I taught her how to throw the weight and hammer one summer. Summer of 2008. I coached her over 40' with the women's weight and close to 130' with the hammer in a summer. I knew I could get you over 35' in the weight over the course of a season," I said with a laugh. "Let's get a little more serious before I have to get back to work. What did you like best about this indoor season?" I asked.

"I liked that you were always honest and up-front with us. You shared your coaching philosophy with us right away. We knew what you were looking for and that you wanted to help us," Luis replied.

"You like how honest I was about that whole class thing?" I asked.

"Yes, even that class thing in the fall. You told me exactly what was going to happen, and it happened."

"Luis, I didn't think that your advisor was going to leave you hanging out to dry like that. I really did think that they would have been better able to help you."

"It's OK now, Coach. I think it worked out really well. It helped me focus on what I needed to do when I came back this spring."

"What do you think I need to work on to be better able to help you this outdoor season? What do you think I need to work on as a coach?"

"This is tough, Coach. Nobody has ever asked me this before. I shouldn't have to critique you."

"Luis, it really is OK. Everyone sharing their thoughts with me will help me become a better coach. If I don't know, then I can't fix anything," I explained. "I had a couple of really bad experiences at Fredonia. I did things that athletes didn't like, and nobody told me. I assumed everyone wanted to throw far, but that wasn't the case. I pushed too hard. I don't want to make the same mistake here."

"What happened at state, Coach?"

"That is a story left to be told another time. Let's get back to you. Never mind old Fredonia stuff," I said. "You already accomplished one of your goals. What do we do now?"

"I try to break the weight record next year?" Luis asked.

"That's not what I really meant. What I mean is that our goals—life goals, college goals, etc.—aren't meant to be written in stone. We can change our minds about things. Maybe you want to change your major, the career you want to pursue, and in your case, who the future Mrs. Rivera will be," I said with a chuckle.

"Coach, that isn't funny. You know that," Luis said.

"Yeah, I know that. You've shared," I said. "And shared, and shared, and shared."

"Yeah, yeah, I get it."

We specifically talked about breaking the hammer record and the discus record.

"I think I have a really good chance to break the hammer record, Coach. I think it's like 110'."

"Luis, you should be able to break it in our first meet. But that shouldn't be the ultimate goal. Luis, you have all the makings of becoming a great thrower. What's cool about throwing is that you ultimately control your own destiny. What you put in is what you'll get out of it. Focus on what you wrote down today, and you'll accomplish everything and then some."

# CHAPTER 29
# THROWING FAR IS NOT EASY TO DO

THE OUTDOOR SEASON, however, did not pick up where the indoor season wrapped up. It took Luis a couple of outdoor competitions to secure a mark in the hammer throw, which would turn out to be his best outdoor event. Luis fouled out of the hammer competition on March 22 and March 30. Our training sessions leading up to those meets were relatively good, but not spectacular.

Luis was having a difficult time making the transition to the hammer throw from the weight throw. Although the technique is exactly the same, the mindset in which you approach the events is somewhat different. Due to the nature of the 35-pound weight throw, some athletes might try to "muscle" the weight out to a far distance. You really can't "muscle" the hammer. It weighs much less and is attached at the end of a 3' wire and handle. It takes more finesse and technical acuity to throw the hammer compared to the weight.

It wasn't until the beginning of April that Luis had a breakthrough in the hammer. Finally figuring out how to fit three heel turns in the circle, he landed his first hammer mark of his collegiate career. On this day in April, Luis finished ninth overall with a mark of 108'1". I knew Luis was disappointed with his performance. It was the only event he threw on that day, and he was competing in front of his friends in our first home meet of the season.

"Luis, nice job today! We got a mark. It's a good start, and you are heading in the right direction," I congratulated.

"Coach, it was horrible. I barely made the finals. And my friends watched. It's embarrassing," remarked Luis.

"What's embarrassing about your performance? You qualified for the finals, you have a mark this year, and now you are eligible to throw at our conference meet."

"It didn't feel good."

"What didn't feel good? Your throw?"

"I don't really know. It just didn't feel right. Throwing doesn't feel right."

"Luis, it's about thirty-five degrees out. I'm freezing. I know you are frozen," I chuckled. "I'm proud of you no matter what you might think about your performance."

"You're proud of that? I barely made the finals."

"Luis, remember when I asked you to write down your goals for the season?"

"Yes, and we've talked about them pretty much every week since."

"Well, I'm glad you aren't sick of discussing them," I said with a wink. "This is all part of the process we've been talking about. Throwing is going to have its ebbs and flows. You haven't really thrown enough to have either, but this is a good start, and you are heading in the right direction."

"I thought I'd be throwing farther by now. I mean, I throw far in practice. Why haven't I thrown well in a meet?"

"Your throwing trajectory this season is high. I'm not sure how high yet. But I think you'll surprise yourself in May. You will ultimately determine how you define your own success. Not me, not your parents, your siblings, professors, anyone. You decide how you define it, and we'll make it happen. I wouldn't sweat at the beginning of April. That won't determine your success. It's a step in our journey together. A step in the right direction."

# CHAPTER 30
# I WASN'T EXPECTING THAT

A FEW WEEKS LATER, Nazareth College hosted the Empire 8 conference championships. It was a cold and windy day, with temperatures in the midthirties. Not an ideal day for throwing in Western New York, but everyone competing that day had to brave the elements. Luis had a couple of good weeks of training leading up to this meet. His discus marks were improving, and his hammer technique was getting more efficient with each successive throw. His confidence was growing as well. I suspected today would be the day that something big would happen; however, it far exceeded what I had imagined.

Coming into this competition, Luis had a personal-best mark of 119'2" in the hammer and 94'7" in the discus. Each practice was getting better, but nothing stood out in practice that would have predicted Luis's performances in each event.

Luis threw the hammer 127'1" to finish fifth overall in the conference. He improved his personal best by almost 10' in the span of two weeks. Huge growth in a relatively short amount of time. That placing secured two points for the men's track team. It was Luis's personal-best throw in the hammer, with four of his six throws surpassing his previous personal best. The winning mark of the day was 142'2".

Luis's hammer mark broke the school record in the process. In the span of four months, with no prior competitive track and field experience, Luis had developed into a competent and competitive thrower in the Empire 8 conference. It wasn't so much his hammer throw that exceeded my expectations but his discus mark. Luis finished second (to Brandon) with a mark of 115'9". If not for Brandon winning the discus competition, Luis would have held both school records on the same day.

"Luis, this is awesome! You scored ten points for your team today. I'm so proud of you!" I exclaimed excitedly. "This is awesome!"

"Thanks, Coach! I wouldn't have been able to do it without you," Luis said.

"Oh, Luis. This is awesome. Two huge personal-best marks with another school record. Congratulations!"

"Thanks, Coach, but we aren't done yet. I think I know what you mean now about setting your expectations higher than what you think you should."

"What do you mean?"

"I mean that I broke the school record in the hammer today and still finished fifth. It isn't about the distances, but all the work that goes into producing those distances. If you would have let me keep my goals to just breaking the school records, I'd be done already. We have a month left this season."

It was at this moment that I was beginning to realize that all the talks, text messages, and emails were indeed helping Luis develop a competitive throwing mindset not only focused on distances and performances but on the process of achieving those results.

Throughout the entire season, I had been sharing daily messages with my throwers that emphasized doing the little things—the boring things that compounded over time would manifest themselves into the big performances they were expecting.

One of my favorite text messages that I often sent everyone was: *Today Is Going to Be a Great Day*. Other text messages I'd send throughout the week were *You Were Meant to Accomplish Great Things*, *I'm Proud of You*, *You Will Shine*, and *There Is Always Something Positive to Take Out of Any Situation*.

I left campus that Saturday afternoon quite impressed with the direction our throwing group was heading. Luis scored ten points for our team. Brandon won the discus and scored in the shot put. He earned the Outstanding Field Performer of the Meet award—an amazing accomplishment for a freshman athlete. Things were trending in a positive direction. Our athletes were beginning to believe in themselves.

The college team traveled roughly six hours to compete in the two-day state championship competition hosted by St. Lawrence University. The hammer and javelin events would be contested on Friday morning, and the shot put and discus would follow on Saturday morning. The team traveled up on Thursday evening.

"There really isn't much more to say, friends. I think everyone is in great shape. I think everyone is ready to throw well. Get a good night's rest, and we'll get at it tomorrow morning," I shared with our thrower group.

I shared how proud I was of everyone and that they should reward themselves with great performances the following two days. I also shared with our throwers that their performances leading up to the meet were very good, and in order to make the finals, they would need to replicate those performances from earlier in the season.

Before calling it for the night, Luis pulled me aside.

"Coach, thank you for everything you've done for me this year," Luis said. "I really appreciate it."

"Luis, it's my pleasure. This is supposed to be fun. Hopefully, we keep the fun going tomorrow," I said with a huge smile on my face.

"Do you think I have a chance to make the finals in the hammer tomorrow?"

"I think you do. I think some things need to happen, but you control the most important part."

"I'm seeded thirteenth out of twenty-four. What do I need to do?"

"Honestly, if you throw over 40m tomorrow, you should be OK. It happens at every meet. We've experienced this before. Those who are seeded the highest don't always live up to their own hype."

"What does that mean, Coach?"

"It means that performing well in competition is one thing, but performing well at conference championships is something different. Your past performances don't always dictate your future outcomes. Everyone starts over at conference and national championships. The top twenty-four coming in won't finish in the same order tomorrow. Yeah, it's great that the others have thrown well, but they haven't thrown well here."

"Yeah, I guess you are right."

"Luis, sometimes things just happen at track meets. It's difficult to explain. You can be seeded number one, but then something happens either before or during the competition. A conversation with a significant other. Someone breaks up with someone. Athletes get nervous. They chase numbers. Chase distances. Anxiety creeps in. You begin to question yourself. It happens. I've seen it happen often."

"Where do you think I'll finish?"

"You'll probably make the finals. For twelve other throwers to all throw just as far tomorrow as they did during the season would be a miracle. I've never coached at a meet where everyone that was supposed to throw far actually did. There are usually three to five throwers who don't throw well. It happens. I think you'll be fine."

"Thanks, Coach. Let's go surprise some people tomorrow!"

# CHAPTER 31
# SURPRISE

It was a beautiful, sunny day in upstate New York. This was the first time I had traveled to this new outdoor complex as a coach. I competed here for both indoor and outdoor competitions as a collegiate athlete, but I had never coached athletes at this outdoor venue. It looked upgraded from the time I competed here almost a decade ago.

Before the start of the competition, I shared a few more thoughts with our throwing group. Luis was the only Nazareth College thrower competing in the hammer. Luis warmed up really well. He was competing in flight one of two. There were twelve throwers in each flight. I figured that Luis would have to throw at least 135' and finish in the top two of his flight in order to qualify for the finals. Because this was a conference meet, the top nine throwers would qualify for the finals.

Luis's first throw of the hammer competition set a new personal best of 137'3" and broke the school record. Luis finished second in the flight, meaning that he needed a lot to happen in flight two in order to make the finals.

"Luis, excellent job," I said as I gave Luis a big hug. "That is a monster throw for your first state conference meet! I'm very proud of you."

"Do you think it's enough to make the finals?"

"It should be. Looking at previous state meet results last night, pretty much everyone who throws as far as you has qualified for the finals. I think you'll be OK."

It was a waiting game. I was sitting attentively in my coaching chair writing down the marks of all the throwers in flight two. I wrote distances, throw after throw. I knew that with five throwers left in the flight, Luis had to beat four of the five in order to qualify for the finals. Luis didn't.

Luis did indeed qualify for the finals! He qualified in the eighth position. He didn't improve his mark from round one, but that wasn't important. What was important to Luis in that moment was that he finished eighth, scored a point for his team, and competed well in a highly stressful and anxiety-inducing competition. Anything less than a personal best on this day would not have qualified Luis for the finals. It was indeed his greatest performance of the outdoor season. The winning throw this day was 173'7". Second place was 149'9", about 12' more than Luis.

"Coach, what do you think," asked Luis as he pointed to the eighth-place medal he was just awarded.

"I think it looks good. The medal looks good, but I think we should switch up the color next year," I said as we shared a big hug on the infield.

"You know, Coach, it wasn't a bad year after all. But you gotta tell me something: Did you think I would be coming back in January?"

"I wasn't sure, to be honest. It wasn't until after New Year's when you shared an Instagram post of you training at the gym. If you weren't coming back, you wouldn't have posted that picture."

"Coach, you didn't think I was coming back. Just be honest," Luis said with a chuckle.

# CHAPTER 32
# A CONFERENCE CHAMPION IN THE MAKING

Fall training went really well for our Nazareth College throwers. We had a large group of male throwers, seven in total. Our total group of throwers was eleven–about the same number of throwers I had at Fredonia.

After our formal first track meeting of the season in early October, I again shared goal-setting sheets with everyone. I also made it a point to meet with each thrower individually to discuss their goals, my expectations, what they expected from me, and anything else that the athlete wanted to share.

I knew we had a good group of male throwers. Nazareth College is arguably one of the best teaching colleges in New York. It wasn't that difficult to recruit athletes, especially if they wanted to major in physical therapy, occupational therapy, or become a speech-language pathologist. Nazareth was then and still is one of the only Division III colleges in the area that offers all three programs.

The last meeting I scheduled was with Luis. We spent a great deal of time talking about training, more purposeful practice, and other areas of his life that he needed to work on in order to better give himself a chance to accomplish his goals.

"All right, Luis," I started, "says here that you want to go to nationals. Tell me about that."

"Coach, I think I can qualify this year. It's only 19'. I think I can do it."

"Luis, 19' is a lot. Let's start with some more realistic numbers before setting our sights on 60'. I think a reasonable number this season would be closer to 55' or 56'. Close to 60' and keeps us working as we get closer. Anything too low might not keep the momentum going."

"Coach, it's only 5' or 6' more feet. Why not just say 60'?"

"I don't want you or myself getting stuck on numbers," I said. "If someone keeps pushing toward a specific number and doesn't get close, motivation and drive tend to fade after a while. But if you say we are going to focus our time and energy on A, B, and C, then eventually we'll get to 60'. You'll get to 60'."

"What do I need to focus on? What will I need to do to get to that level?"

"I think we'll need to be more purposeful about your training. Not waste throws in practice. Pick one or two technical cues to focus on during the week and master them before we move on to the next one. We won't have much time to take a lot of throws this indoor season. We'll need to be more mindful about the quality of your throws, and not necessarily the volume."

"Anything else?"

"Well, we got your grades and things figured out. I think we should be OK there. Definitely think more about recovery from training. We have a great athletic training staff and sauna. Sit in the ice bath after practice for a few minutes. Rest in the sauna. Try to get at least seven hours of sleep a night. These are all little things that add up over time that will make it easier for you to accomplish your goals."

"Seven hours a night is a lot, Coach. What about all my homework?"

"Listen, be honest with yourself. I know you are not doing homework at two, three, and four o'clock in the morning when you are sending me Instagram videos of people lifting and throwing. You'll feel so much better when you consistently get more sleep and don't stay out as much."

From all my past coaching and training experiences, it was indeed the mundane activities that would eventually determine what Luis achieved this season. Doing boring things well over a repeated amount of time would lay the foundation from which he would reach the peak of his Mount Everest.

We had a great fall semester of training! Where last season Luis was a predominantly one-turn weight thrower, we transitioned to two turns for the weight. Two turns would allow him to generate more momentum and speed in the circle, which in turn would hopefully lead to a greater release velocity and longer throws. We didn't take many weight throws during the week. We had limited space and a limited amount of time. We were quickly outgrowing our auxiliary gym. We had a lot of throwers and not as much space as we had in the past. My work schedule did not allow me the additional time to be there longer, and with a little one at home, I didn't want to spend three hours at practice.

Luis had made a nice transition to a one-wind and two-turn technique. He was getting more fluid and comfortable in the circle. I knew it. Luis didn't realize it until one day in training before

Thanksgiving break. We were throwing across the auxiliary gym and Luis hit a monster throw that almost clipped the bottom of the backboard across from us. It was a big throw! At least 40' to hit the bottom of the backboard.

"Luis, it looks like things are really coming together. That was huge!" I exclaimed. "You are definitely ready for Brockport."

"You think so, Coach? That was a good throw?"

"Luis, that is a big throw. You almost got us permanently kicked out of here. If you break that backboard, someone is going to be really upset with us. I think you are ready for the meet."

## CHAPTER 33

# WELCOME TO THE 50' CLUB

IT WAS A SHORT DRIVE DOWN TO BROCKPORT. I thought Luis was very well prepared for the meet. We had a great series of training sessions leading up to the meet. Our strategy for the meet was to feel comfortable in the circle with two-turn throws. That was basically it. We weren't going to drop down to one-turn throws, because in the long run that would hurt his technique more than help. Yes, making the finals is good, and being able to take a monster one-turn throw would be nice, but in the long run, a one-turn throw wouldn't get us where we wanted to go: nationals.

Luis ended up finishing fourth overall in a strong field of competitors early on in the season. He set a personal best with a throw of 47'4.5". The winning throw came from a Brockport senior at 51'5".

"Luis, nice start to the season. Four big throws over your old personal best. I like how you went after it in rounds five and six," I said. "Really nice work."

"Thanks, Coach, but there is still more in there. I know I can compete with these guys. I'll be ready for RIT next week."

Luis was indeed ready for this competition, although I was

concerned at the onset because James (Nazareth head coach) allowed some of the athletes to drive themselves to this Friday-evening meet. Athletes were instructed to be at the meet one hour before their competition. Luis and Brandon drove together but missed the one-hour deadline. They also missed weigh-ins. That meant they would be using another team's implements for the competition because our throwing implements weren't certified. I was concerned. And upset. Not their typical behavior.

As the first flight of the competition began, in strolled Luis and Brandon. I was coaching our other male throwers but caught them coming in out of the corner of my eye. I was upset with them. When we initially made eye contact, I could sense that something was up with Luis. Before I made my way over to speak to him, he was intercepted by James. I'm not sure what he said to Luis, but I didn't need to follow up. James usually played bad cop; I played good cop.

"Thanks for coming, guys. I was concerned you wouldn't make it," I said.

"Sorry we're late, Coach," Brandon replied.

"Were you busy doing some homework? What happened?"

"Don't worry about it now, Coach," Luis replied. "I don't want to talk about it."

I left it at that. I'm sure James said something to them about being late, being irresponsible, and all that comes with that. Now it was my turn to pick them up and get them ready to compete.

"OK, Luis. You are in the last flight. You have some time to warm up. But we'll continue with what we started at Brockport. Bring the heat in the early rounds and put pressure on everyone else," I said.

"Don't worry about it, Coach. I'll take care of it."

Luis put his headphones on and walked away. I thought that was odd. He usually enjoyed having conversations right up until it was time to warm up. He sat down in one of the lounge chairs I often brought to meets. He put on his headphones and put his head down. I remember thinking to myself that it was either going to be a good day or bad day. No in-between with this one. It was either going to be a personal-best day, or we were going to flame out.

Luis did not flame out. Luis finished second with a monster throw of 50'5.25! A huge improvement from just a few days prior, and this throw also qualified him for the East Coast Athletic Conference (ECAC) championship meet in early March. When the mark was read aloud, I screamed in excitement at the top of my lungs! I didn't believe such a big throw would come so soon in the season. Luis also became the first male thrower who I coached over the 50' mark in the weight throw.

"Luis, welcome to the 50' club!" I exclaimed. "This is such an amazing accomplishment. You've added almost 9' to your personal best this season. Very well earned and deserved!"

We had a lot to celebrate, but there was also a lot more work to be done. Luis was beginning to feel more comfortable in the circle. It wouldn't become a hurdle until later in the season, but Luis was beginning to notice that there wasn't going to be much competition around our area for him. Many of the other throwers in the area were rather sporadic, throwing really well one week and then missing the finals the next. There were a couple of tests we were going to run into in the spring semester.

Our winter session block of training went really well. With Luis living in Rochester, he was able to train at Nazareth College over winter break. He still maintained quite a demanding work schedule at Wegmans, but he didn't miss one training session. Of all our throwers, he came back from break in the best shape.

# CHAPTER 34
# THROWING WITH OLYMPIANS

One of the meets immediately after our break took place at the newly opened SPIRE Institute in Geneva, Ohio. This facility maintains the status of an Olympic training center, and as Division III athletes, we were able to compete at their facility. This would be a different kind of competition for Luis. Our strategy leading up to this meet would be to focus on a solid and confident entry into his weight throw. We had been working on different technical cues to support this subtle change and thought it would be a good time to unleash it onto the world here in Ohio.

The athletes and I competing at this meet were graced with the presence of three-time American hammer thrower A. G. Kruger. A. G. was coming off the 2012 Olympic Games, was sponsored by Nike, and was using this meet as his indoor season opener.

When I was a fairly competitive hammer thrower myself between 2006 and 2010, I frequented many meets in the state of Ohio and competed against A. G. Kruger. On this day, he was accompanied by the Canadian record holder in the hammer, Derek Woodske.

I'm not sure if anyone else realized that A. G. would be competing at this meet, but when I saw his name listed on the entry list, I knew it was going to be a great learning experience for Luis, our Nazareth throwers, and the other throwers attending the competition. As AG was getting settled, I went over and greeted Derek with a handshake and hug. We made some small talk for about twenty minutes before I waved over my athletes and introduced them to Derek.

"Guys, this is Derek Woodske. He is the Canadian record holder in the hammer and arguably one of the best 35-pound weight throwers in history. He is also the coach who wrote the beef-packers edition strength and conditioning program," I said.

All the athletes recognized Derek from some of the throwing videos I had previously sent them about focus and confidence. Over the years, I'd begun posting a lot of old throwing videos on YouTube for the world to enjoy. In most of the videos, you'll see Derek throwing the weight at Kent State in 2006 and 2007, where he used a two-turn technique to throw the weight 80' and lead the world.

I said hello to AG, but I didn't want to interrupt his precompetition routine, but I pointed out what he was doing to Luis.

"Luis, that is A. G. Kruger. Just came off the 2012 Olympic Games. Looks like he is warming up like you do," I shared. "This will be a good opportunity for you to learn. You are competing today against a three-time Olympic thrower. Doesn't get much better than this. It's like a fantasy camp for throwers."

"Fantasy camp," Luis said quizzically. "What does that mean?"

"Well, it means there really aren't that many sports in which someone can compete against someone else who has represented the United States at the Olympics. We would never be able to get on the football field with Tom Brady. But here we are with arguably the two best weight throwers of the past decade. You are going to throw against AG. You aren't going to compete against other high-profile athletes like this in baseball, basketball, or hockey. But here we are among the greats of the throwing world."

Another nice aspect about throwing in Ohio was that Luis would be competing against arguably the best Division III thrower in history, Sean Donnelly. Sean was competing for Mount Union and was a returning national champion thrower. Sean had earned All-American status in the hammer throw, weight throw, and shot put events. He had won multiple national championships, and up until the 2022–2023 season, he held the Division III weight throw record and championship meet record.

In this star-studded field of throwers, Luis threw a modest 48'8.25" to finish in fifth place. Statistically, it was the best meet of his career, but what bothered him most was that he didn't set a personal best.

"Coach, I didn't have it today," Luis said dejectedly. "I'm sorry."

"Luis, you never have to apologize for your performances. Some meets are better than others. The wins for this meet are that you didn't foul any throws, and statistically this was your best meet of the season. And you threw against A. G. Doesn't get much better than that."

"I could have set a personal best, Coach," Luis said.

"Yes, you could have. That would have moved you up to fourth place. Would that make you that much happier?"

# CHAPTER 35
# FIRST STEPS TOWARD GREATNESS

THE FOLLOWING WEEK WE RETURNED to Ithaca College for the Empire 8 indoor conference championship meet. Luis and I had high expectations for this meet. Many of the top throwers from last season had graduated, and Luis was seeded as the top-ranked thrower in the competition. On paper, it was the best group of male throwers I had coached in my brief career. We had a really good chance of taking the top two spots in the men's weight throw and also scoring in the shot put.

"Luis, what do you think? Open like we did a few weeks ago? Big throw in round one and put the competition away early?" I said with a chuckle. This phrase had turned into an inside joke between Luis and I based on a YouTube video we watched a few weeks prior.

"You know it, Coach. Always sending big throws early," Luis responded.

In a situation like this, I often encouraged my top-ranked throwers to try to enter the competition with an up-tempo throw, meaning a throw that is roughly 95 percent of their best effort, which would leave an impression on the rest of the competition. Reflecting on my time at Fredonia, I always felt timid going into the competition seeded first. In learning from my mistakes of throwing to not lose, I encouraged Luis to throw to win as if he were chasing others. I remember Jud Logan sharing something similar in a conference video I watched. He shared a story about encouraging his best athletes to hit big throws early and then really go for the win in the following rounds.

Luis threw in the second flight, and indeed went for an up-tempo throw in round one. It went all of 38' and change. Not the way we wanted to start the competition. I pulled him aside after the throw to impart some wisdom.

"Luis, we got that one out of your system. Round one isn't going to hurt us. Let's pick it up in round two," I said.

Luis was looking at me, but I'm not sure how much he absorbed.

Our outcome in round two was much different: 47'3.75". This throw propelled Luis into first place, where he would remain for the remainder of the competition. The second-place finisher had a throw of 47'. The competition was much closer than I initially anticipated, but it showed that even on one of his worst throwing days of the season, it was still better than everyone else's best day.

"Congratulations, Luis! Your first conference championship. I'm really proud of you!" I exclaimed.

"Thank you, Coach. It feels good to be a conference champion. It was closer than I thought it was going to be," Luis said.

"It shows that your worst throw of the season so far is still that much better than everyone else's best throw of the season. A win is a win, Luis. Not many people ask how far, but what was the result."

Our focus leading up to the indoor state meet was to continue building upon Luis's comfort level in the circle and increasing the intensity of his early-round throws. I knew that the next couple of meets, including states and ECACs, would require Luis to throw big marks early on in the competition to ensure a shot in qualifying for the finals.

Over the course of the next two meets, February 15 at Ithaca and February 21 at RIT, Luis increased his personal best in the weight throw. At Ithaca, Luis finished fifth, with a throw of 51'8" and 52'1.25" for a fourth-place finish at RIT.

His throws were trending in the right direction. Most importantly, Luis was feeling more confident and beginning to act more like the amazing thrower he was growing into. Luis didn't become arrogant, but rather he started treating throwing more seriously. He was doing really well in school, and he started spending more of his free time focused on throwing—watching throwing videos, engaging with other throwers on social media, and tracking everything in his journal.

I think Luis realized he had a really good chance to become a great thrower. Great will be defined differently. Everyone has their own definition of what great is. Great can be defined by growth. Great can be defined by outcomes. Great can be defined by a combination of both. We defined great by growth.

A couple of days before the state meet, Luis and I were walking down to the weight room after a throwing session.

"Luis, the state meet is in a couple of days. What do you think about it?" I asked.

"It's going to be a different outcome than last year, Coach. I'm not messing around this year," Luis responded.

"I know you aren't, Luis. I know you are taking this more seriously this year. You are beginning to act the part of a great thrower.

Like I always talk about, everyone starts over at these big meets. It doesn't matter where someone is seeded. Only outcomes performed here at states matter. I think you are ready to leave your mark on the conference this weekend."

"You think I have a chance of placing?" Luis asked. "How do you think I'll finish?"

In the couple of seconds, I had to respond. I knew I had to be mindful of my response. Up to this point, I had always shared my honest thoughts about performances and outcomes with my athletes. I never wanted to tell them they would have great days in fear of failure and thus negatively affecting my relationship with our throwers. I didn't want to aim too low for fear of the athletes thinking I didn't believe in them. It was a difficult balance of how much praise was too much without overinflating expectations for a great performance.

"Luis, I think you are going to throw well. I think you'll surprise yourself with a nice performance, and if you throw like you have the past couple of weeks, you'll certainly make the finals. Then you'll be throwing with house money," I said. "You are seeded in the top half of the qualified throwers. As long as you throw what got you into the meet, you'll be OK."

A response like this would become my go-to conversation if I had any doubts. Luis had thrown really well the past couple of weeks. We hadn't hit a streak of three consecutive solid performances. Setting a personal best in three consecutive weeks is difficult, especially at the point Luis was reaching. He wasn't elite yet by any stretch. He was very competitive, but a lot of his peers were throwing in the low 50' range. Anyone could have a great day and set a personal best and bump him down. A few athletes could hit big marks and move him down. What I was learning as a coach was that if an athlete hit a mark within 95 percent of their best performance of the season in the championship meet, there was a really good chance they would qualify for the finals. It didn't happen all the time, but performing close to a personal best at least gave you a chance. Falling off at 85–90 percent would not guarantee a chance at qualifying for the finals.

We drove up to St. Lawrence on Thursday night after our athletes finished their classes. We stopped for dinner halfway to our destination. We didn't have a lot of athletes competing, but the ones who were had really good chances for qualifying for the ECAC meet and scoring points at this state meet. I didn't share much with Luis on Thursday night. We had dinner, discussed classes, and talked about our strategy for the meet.

"Luis, let's continue as we have been this season. Let's go in with a big up-tempo throw in round one and see what happens," I said.

"You know it, Coach. We are bringing heat in round one this year," Luis responded confidently.

Luis brought that confidence into the meet. Luis warned up really well and almost hit a personal best in round one. In fact, his round-one performance was good enough to seed Luis first going into the finals. Luis set a personal best in round four. A competitor from RPI also hit a personal best, throwing just under 53'. Luis reclaimed the top spot in round five with another personal best, throwing 53'3.5". The RPI thrower also hit a personal best, finishing with a throw of 54'0". Luis had a chance to win the competition in round six, as he was the last thrower to take an attempt. He went for it, but unfortunately fouled his attempt. In one year, Luis went from fouling out of the state meet to finishing second and breaking up an RPI sweep (athletes finishing first, second, and third).

"Luis, this is amazing! Congratulations. You went for it big in the finals, and look what happened—amazing things," I said in excitement. "I'm so proud of you!"

As I sat in my coaching chair after watching this competition, I couldn't help but think to myself that Luis was someday going to qualify for nationals and probably become an All-American. He was composed in this high-stress and anxiety-causing situation. He set two personal-best throws in the finals, all while controlling his emotions and remaining composed. Other throwers might have wilted under the situation, but Luis rose up to the occasion. He had two marks over 16m, had five fair throws, and had his best meet-throwing average of the season. Everything came together in this one meet at St. Lawrence. From never having thrown just eighteen months earlier, Luis was blossoming into a very good thrower.

# CHAPTER 36
# NOTHING BUT PERSONAL-BEST THROWS

Our outdoor season picked up right where the indoor season wrapped up. Even though Luis did not perform to his expectations at the ECAC meet held in Boston, Luis used that performance to refocus on his goals for the outdoor season.

I knew Luis was going to make a successful transition to the hammer throw. He was comfortable with his technique with the weight, and adding a third hammer turn didn't faze him. Similar to last year, we spent a majority of the outdoor season practicing in the snow. Most days we had a couple of inches of snow on the ground, which made practice rather uncomfortable, but I kept assuring Luis that everyone around the Northeast was also practicing outside in the snow.

In our first three outdoor meets of the season, Luis set a personal best in the hammer throw, upping his personal best to 157'5" before our Empire 8 outdoor championships. He didn't win any of our first three meets, but he qualified for the finals in each competition and upped his meet average along the way.

St. John Fisher College hosted our outdoor conference championship meet. Even though our schools are essentially on the same road separated by less than a mile in distance, we didn't compete here early on in the season. Luis was the top-seeded hammer thrower heading into the competition. Something that he was proud of.

"Coach, we are going to run this back. Win both the weight and the hammer. What do you think?" Luis asked confidently.

"I think you have a really good chance of winning and joining some nice company of previous throwers who had won the double in the same season—35-pound weight and hammer. I don't think it's happened in a while. Probably time for someone to do it," I shared.

Unlike our previous three meets, Luis had his worst performance of the season at this meet. He threw the hammer 142'8". He barely made it into the finals and had to work during his final three throws of the competition. In between the prelims and finals, I pulled him aside to chat.

"Well, what a situation we have here. You barely sneaked into the finals, my friend. Let's bring the heat in round four and see what happens," I said.

"Coach, I might lose," Luis said.

"Well, if you throw the way you have been, you aren't going to win either. Bring the heat and see what happens."

Luis brought the heat in round four. Right into the cage. Even in situations like this, Luis never seemed fazed. He still carried himself confidently on the outside, but it took me another year to figure out what was going on inside when he was in situations like this. Round five was our saving grace. Luis hit his best throw of the competition, 145'9", and beat the second-place competitor by 7'. Much closer than we both anticipated, but Luis was able to pull it off again. Having picked our two conference meets to throw his worst distances of the season, Luis did indeed pull off the 35-pound weight and hammer throw double.

"You wanted to add a little drama to the competition today?" I asked with a chuckle. "This was a close one, my friend, but you pulled it off, given the situation. Another impressive performance."

"Coach, this was horrible. I should have won by 15'. It was too close," Luis said.

"That's OK. You won. You won again. Winning in these types of circumstances now is going to help you later. Adversity builds character in competition. Maybe it's not the distance we thought you would hit, but a win is a win. Second of the season," I said.

"I'm a double champion, Coach. The champ champ," Luis said proudly.

"Yes, Luis. The champ champ, indeed," I responded.

Luis turned his whole season around after our conference championship meet. He had three successive meets over 162' in the hammer, setting a personal best in two of three meets. Similar to the meets leading up to our conference meet, Luis didn't win any of these meets, but he increased his meet average in each successive meet. I always managed to find a silver lining in our track and field meets. There was always something to celebrate—a win that would help build up the confidence of our athletes.

Luis had his best statistical meet of the season at the outdoor state meet. Finding ourselves throwing at St. John Fisher College again, Luis finished third in the hammer throw with a distance of 162'11"—3" under his personal best from the previous week. The winner from RPI threw 181'. Luis broke up a potential first through fourth sweep by RPI. It wasn't his hammer mark that I was as impressed with, but his discus mark. Luis set a personal best in the discus with a throw of 130'7", good enough for seventh place and two points for our Nazareth College team. A different RPI thrower won the discus with a mark of 151'8".

Luis had put together quite a successful sophomore season. He won two conference championships, set a multitude of personal-best throws in the weight throw, hammer throw, and discus throw. He was Nazareth College's school record holder in the weight throw, hammer throw, and discus throw. He also competed in both the indoor and outdoor ECAC championship meets.

I wasn't quite sure how the ECAC meet was going to go. Luis was throwing in the first flight of two. Each flight had twelve throwers. It was going to be difficult to make it to the finals, but the way Luis was throwing, I thought there would be a good chance he would make the finals.

It was my first visit to RPI's campus in Troy, New York. It was a rather warm day for mid-May in Western New York. I wasn't able to travel with the team. After I wrapped up at school, I drove three hours for the competition.

In round two of the prelims, Luis set a personal-best mark in the hammer with a distance of 166'6". It was a big mark, his first time over the 50m barrier. With that throw in round two, Luis finished second in the flight of twelve.

"Luis, as always, I'm very proud of you. Another personal best. We are going to wait and see what happens in the second flight. Have a seat and be ready. You never know what is going to happen."

It was a long wait. But as Luis and I had discussed many times during the season, you never knew what would happen in high-stress, high anxiety-causing throwing situations. Some throwers performed really well in the second flight. Others, not so much. Not so much, in fact, that Luis barely qualified for the finals. He went into the finals as the last thrower. He went into finals as the ninth thrower, and he finished the competition in ninth place. Both the first- and second-place finishers threw over 200'. The winning mark at 216'5". The top two throwers at this meet went on to earn All-American status at nationals by finishing in the top eight in the country. It was probably the most competitive ECAC men's hammer competition in history. Third place was 197', and fourth place was 180'2". The top three throwers threw over 60m. It was the first time in my coaching career that I watched that many collegiate throwers throw over 60m.

There isn't much more I can say about Luis's sophomore season. Personal-best marks across the board. Two conference championships. And a finals appearance at ECACs. His season couldn't have been written much better. The throwing rocket ship was strapped to his back. He was primed to have an even more successful junior season.

# CHAPTER 37
# EARNING YOUR DOCTORATE IS HARD WORK

I ENJOYED MY TIME AS AN ASSISTANT track and field coach. The only negative part of coaching was the time away from my wife and son. I wasn't very helpful when I was home, because I was always thinking about coaching and throwing. It wasn't fair to my wife. It certainly wasn't fair to Joseph. In early June I asked James to meet and discuss the upcoming 2014–2015 season.

James and I met in his office in early June. I had made the decision to step away from coaching. It was taking up a lot of time. It didn't help that my salary for the year was around $1,000. The money was nice because I enjoyed what I was doing, but it wasn't helpful at home. I spent a lot of time on Nazareth's campus. I was enjoying my job at the Volunteers of America Children's Center and couldn't keep taking time off from work to travel for track meets, especially if there wasn't going to be much of an opportunity to pursue coaching as a full-time endeavor. I told James I appreciated the opportunity he provided me two years ago and that I wanted to spend more time at home. He understood and I parted ways with Nazareth College on good terms.

I haven't mentioned it yet, but all through the 2013–2014 season, I had stepped back into the world of powerlifting. After I graduated from Fredonia in 2004, I began training for powerlifting competitions. I had a string of successful competitions from December 2004 to March 2006. I broke a couple of New York State United States of America Powerlifting (USAPL) federation records in the 242-pound and 275-pound classes. I held junior records (20–23 years old) in the 242-pound squat, bench, and total as well as the squat, bench, and total in the 275-pound weight class. I also qualified for USAPL nationals. After I recovered from my right tricep tendon surgery in June 2012, I thought it would have been a good idea to start training for powerlifting competitions again.

If you couldn't tell, I'm a goal-oriented person. I always feel as though I need to be doing something to become a better version of myself. Powerlifting filled a void in my life. Now that I was older, I needed to be smarter about my training, but it was a challenge that I looked forward to facing again.

There was something else I had always wanted to accomplish in my life. Something I wrote about in my goal journal a long time ago. I always wanted to earn my doctorate in education. Back in April 2008, I wrote that one of my bucket list items was to secure a tenure-track teaching position at a college and also coach at the same college. I had figured out the coaching part, but I was obviously missing the doctorate. St. John Fisher College offered an accelerated EdD program in executive leadership. I had previously applied to the University of Rochester's PhD program in both psychology and education. I applied three times and made it to an interview in the summer of 2013, but was never accepted into their programs.

In early July 2014, Laura encouraged me to apply to St. John Fisher College's program. I went to one of their program sessions in the middle of July. I met the department chair and a couple of professors in the program. I didn't ask any questions, but I introduced myself to the chair and professors who attended.

The following day I sent all three of them emails thanking them for their time and that I was interested in applying to earn acceptance into their Cohort 9 that would be starting in August 2014. One of the professors, Dr. Montes, suggested I apply and told me that he thought I would be a good candidate for their next cohort.

In early August 2014, I completed my application to earn acceptance into St. John Fisher College's EdD program in executive leadership. A week later I was called to come in for an interview. I accepted and met with the chair and one additional professor. I had never been more nervous in my life. Unlike my interview at the University of Rochester, I thought I actually had a chance to gain acceptance into this program.

We met for over an hour. I was asked a variety of questions focused on leadership, my teaching philosophy, and my education philosophy as a whole. I did my best to answer the questions despite my limited prior leadership experience. I answered many of the questions from the perspective of a coach, which is not that much different from a leadership position. In both roles, you are leading a group of individuals toward accomplishing a specific goal—or so I thought at the time. At the conclusion of the interview, I thanked both of them for their time. I called Laura from the parking lot and told her that I thought the interview went well and that they would tell me within a week if I was accepted into the program.

It was difficult to focus at the VOA while I waited for the call letting me know if I had been accepted. While waiting for the response from Fisher, I competed in a local powerlifting meet in Rochester, New York. Luis competed as well, and it was a bit awkward. I had told him a few weeks prior that I was not returning. He did not take the news well. He was upset, and he shared with me why he was upset. What made things awkward at the powerlifting meet was that I had encouraged him to compete as a way to train and get ready for the start of the 2014–2015 season. I finished second overall in my weight class and also had the second biggest total of the meet. A total is when you add the weight of your best squat, bench, and deadlift. There is a formula that I'm not that familiar with that is implemented to determine the best lifter of the meet regardless of body weight. I had the third best meet of those who competed. I didn't set a personal best in any of the three lifts, but I had fun, was leaving the meet healthy, and had qualified for the federations national championships, which would be taking place later in 2015.

A couple of days after the powerlifting meet, I received a letter in the mail from Fisher.

"Laura, open the letter and tell me what it says," I said nervously. "Hopefully, I got accepted."

Laura opened the letter and read it aloud to me.

"Dear Charles, congratulations on your acceptance into DEXL's EdD program in executive leadership," Laura shared.

"Laura, I can't believe it. I'm going to start working on my doctorate. This is going to help us so much when I'm done," I said excitedly.

The program was accelerated in nature, unlike other doctorate programs. Courses were offered in cohort format over a duration of twenty-eight months. With all things going well, I would be graduating from the DEXL program in May 2017.

A couple of days after I was accepted, I completed my FAFSA form online. This program would introduce a large financial investment for Laura and me. Money that we didn't have at the time. I would end up borrowing money to cover the cost for the whole program, over $100,000 after all was said and done. I was set to begin classes at the end of August 2014. Starting my doctorate program was not the only new challenge I would be experiencing. A week before classes started, Laura shared that we were pregnant and would be introducing a new person into the world in May 2015.

In the span of a couple of weeks, I had resigned from a coaching position that I was enjoying but taking too much time away from my family, qualified for a national championship powerlifting meet, been accepted into a doctorate program, went through financial counseling that Fisher offered, and found out that we would be welcoming a new person into this world in May 2015. I don't remember sharing with Laura that I had this heightened sense of overwhelm, but I felt it on the inside. It was quite a summer.

It is critically important to mention that I was no longer coaching at Nazareth College; therefore I was no longer Luis's throwing coach. Luis and I texted every once and a while during the season, but nothing of substance. I cannot speak to his successes over the course of his junior season, but I will summarize at the conclusion of this section.

I didn't really know what I was going to focus my attention on in my doctorate work. Classes were every other Friday night from 6:00 p.m. to 9:00 p.m. and Saturday from 9:00 a.m. to 4:00 p.m. Essentially, we completed two courses per semester plus a field experience class for credit but not for a grade. I was still working at the VOA and thought I should try to tie some of my doctorate work into the work I was already doing to support Head Start. I only shared the news of being accepted in the doctorate program with my director supervisor, Rob, and the VOA president and vice president.

Classes were much different than I had anticipated. Most of our class time on Friday night was spent discussing our assignments, what was happening in the news, and how current events were tied to leadership styles and communication skills. We sat in groups we were assigned to on the first night. I was paired with Rachel Santiago. She was a professor at MCC and a math wiz. We were paired together that first night of class in August 2014 and sat next to each other throughout the rest of the program until we graduated in May 2017.

Early on our assignments were focused on leadership, leadership styles, and how we as individuals would attend to certain situations based on our own philosophy on leading. I didn't really have much experience leading adults, so a lot of the experiences I referred to in class were about coaching collegiate athletes. I considered it out-of-the-box thinking, because if you could lead a group of college athletes on one common path, it wouldn't be that much different than leading adults in the same direction. This theory was incorrect. At the time, I thought the situations were similar, but they couldn't be further away from each other. I kept to my stories about coaching. Others shared their experiences in the field of education and business.

I earned an A and an A- in my first semester of doctorate work. I hadn't really tied anything to my work with the VOA and Head Start. I was really trying to figure out if I was going to move into the direction of early childhood education or athletics. I was at a crossroads in my life. The decision to pick one or the other would essentially impact the rest of my professional career and the life Laura and I were beginning to build. I spent some time in the fall working with a professor from Brockport. His research focused on ethics in athletics, which seemed interesting to me at the time.

The North Carolina athletics department and academic department scandal was breaking, and it seemed like a path I could take. I gave a presentation in December 2014 on the positive effects early childhood programming had on later school outcomes, and when asked if this was the direction I wanted to continue pursuing, I answered my professor with a resounding no. I shared with my cohort that I was going to move forward with something in the field of athletics. That changed a few weeks later.

# CHAPTER 38
# A DECISION TODAY AFFECTS YOUR LIFE TOMORROW

I WAS SITTING IN MY OFFICE AT THE VOA in January 2015 when I received a call from my doctorate advisor, Guillermo Montes. Dr. Montes told me that the team at Fisher was meeting to pick my dissertation committee and that they wanted to know if I was going to move forward with athletics or early childhood education. I asked him if I could think about it for a day or two and call him back. He said I needed to decide now, at that moment. I blurted out that I wanted to focus on early childhood education. He said OK and hung up. It wasn't what I wanted to do. I picked that subject because I thought it would best help my family in the long run.

In the spring of 2015, I officially began working on a dissertation focused on early childhood education. I didn't have a specific topic, or pinhole, as it was often referred to by our professors. My role at the VOA was as the education and disability specialist in collaboration with Head Start. I was responsible for approximately 250 preschool students who were enrolled in our building. Even though

I was an employee of the VOA, I spent quite a bit of time working with my Head Start peers in Rochester. I thought it would probably be a good idea to pick a topic that I dealt with every day and could support the work that I was already doing.

My dissertation topic selection process was accelerated in the spring of 2015 because we had to fulfill a field experience portion of a course that was associated with our dissertation topic. Dr. Montes suggested I call a gentleman by the name of Dirk Hightower. At the time, he was the executive director of the Children's Institute, a not-for-profit organization associated with the University of Rochester whose focus was to support the social-emotional well-being of young children. Dr. Montes told me that Dirk's expertise was centered on quality early childhood programming and student academic outcomes. I was intrigued, but I was not yet convinced this topic would dictate the rest of my professional career.

It took me until early February to finally have a conversation with Dirk. I met him in his office at the Children's Institute. As I was walking down the main hallway, I caught a glimpse of Dr. Montes. What I would soon find out was that Dr. Montes was the coresearch director at the Children's Institute. What I didn't realize until then was that Dr. Montes was trying to point me in the right direction—or at least a direction.

Dirk and I met for about an hour. I shared with him a *Reader's Digest* version of my professional career and what I thought I wanted to be when I grew up. I told Dirk that I was interested in learning more about program quality and its relationship to student outcomes in preschool classrooms. Earlier in the week, I read an article about classroom quality and its effects on student outcomes as they transition from preschool to kindergarten. I was familiar with the program quality assessment tool because I had become a trained classroom assessment scoring system (CLASS) scorer. The CLASS is a research-based early childhood observational assessment tool that is used to inform best practices in preschool settings. I wanted to examine the relationship between the program quality of Rochester preschool classrooms and if the quality of the programmatic environment had an effect on student learning. He agreed to support this research project and also agreed to become my mentor for the field experience.

I spent the rest of the spring semester learning as much as I could about the CLASS and student outcomes in preschool programming. This work allowed me to sit in with a group of individuals who met every other Thursday at the Children's Institute. The team known as RECAP met to discuss early childhood programming in the Rochester City School District. There were fourteen members on the team. I was able to sit in on meetings beginning in early March. I just sat, listened, and took notes of things I thought were interesting or that I had more questions about. I was kind of considered an outsider, and I was told that what happens in Vegas, stays in Vegas. There was nothing of note that I would have shared with my VOA peers anyway. I was just happy to be there.

Dirk and I met every couple of weeks to discuss my progress and if I had any questions about the project. I didn't know anything about statistical packages besides being able to write some basic Excel programs. Dirk was showing me all sorts of things related to statistical code writing. I was a quick learner and was taught enough to complete my project and give a presentation about it in class. I did such a nice job that when a position became available at the Children's Institute, I asked Dirk if I should apply. I asked for a couple of reasons. First, I was going to be in need of a job really soon because I was told by Rob at the VOA that I would not be coming back after June 30. My job was being combined with another position, and they would not need me anymore. The conversation I had with Rob had me feeling extremely nervous and scared about my future. Laura and I were expecting in May, and in late March, I was told I wouldn't be coming back to my job in July. Second, I was becoming really interested in my classroom quality and student outcome work. I enjoyed working with Dirk. I was beginning to develop a rapport with other individuals at the Children's Institute, and I would be gaining employment at the University of Rochester.

I officially started working at the Children's Institute on June 22, 2015. My official title was information analyst. I was assigned to the RECAP project. It was an exciting turn in my professional career. I was really excited about the topic centered around early childhood program quality. I didn't realize it at the time, but I had a gold mine of data, allowing me to answer research questions and eventually publish peer-reviewed research articles.

While all this was going on in my professional life, Luis was in the midst of completing a remarkable junior season. As I was sitting in class all spring semester, Luis was setting the Northeast throwing world on fire. Luis defended his Empire 8 indoor weight throw championship by hitting a meet record throw of 60'6". He finished second at the indoor state meet with a throw of 59'11.75". Most remarkable of all for his indoor season was that Luis finished sixth at the Division III 2015 indoor national championships in the 35-pound weight throw with a monster throw of 63'3.50". That throw not only set the Nazareth College school record but the Empire 8 conference record as well.

Luis did not rest on his indoor laurels, however. He kept the momentum going through the outdoor season by again defending his Empire 8 hammer championship with a throw of 166'4". He won the outdoor state meet hammer championship by hitting a throw of 187'11", which also broke the Empire 8 conference record in the hammer throw. His throw of 187'11" qualified him for the Division III outdoor national championships in the hammer throw. Luis entered the competition as the twentieth-seeded thrower out of twenty in the men's hammer. Depending on the narrative you'd like to write about the situation, Luis defied the odds and ended up finishing with another personal-best performance of 192'2", good enough for an eighth-place finish and another All-American certificate. When I saw the results of the hammer competition, I sent Luis a congratulatory text message.

"Luis, congrats on an amazing season. I'm very proud of you and all that you accomplished this year. Best wishes on an even more amazing senior season!"

Luis quickly texted back. "I couldn't have done it without you, Coach. Everything you taught me the past couple of years helped me get through nationals. Thank you."

It really was an amazing accomplishment. Since his freshman season, Luis had added 20' to his personal best in the 35-pound weight throw and close to 50' in the hammer throw. Really remarkable growth for someone so new to the sport. He completed a magical season.

## CHAPTER 39

# BRINGING THE BAND BACK TOGETHER

IN LATE JUNE 2015, Luis started sending me text messages about possibly coming back to coach at Nazareth College for the 2015–2016 season. I thought it was odd since he already had a throwing coach and didn't really make much of it until he called me before the Fourth of July.

"Coach, I want you to come back to Nazareth College," Luis started. "The coach we had this past season is going to be leaving. They are posting the job soon, and I want you to apply."

"Luis, that sounds really nice, but you have someone. They haven't posted anything yet," I said.

"Believe me. They will be posting the job soon, and I want you to coach me through my senior year."

"Well, if the job is posted, I'll apply. But I cannot make any promises. I have one year to go in my doctorate work, and I have two littles at home. We'll have to see what happens," I said.

"Don't worry about it, Coach. When the job is posted, just apply.

I'll take care of the rest."

I shared this news with Laura later on in the afternoon. I expressed to her my interest in the position, what Luis had accomplished during his junior season, and what his senior year could look like.

"Laura, this could be a once-in-a-lifetime opportunity. From what I've looked at online, Luis is the top returning weight thrower in the country. He is also the fifth-ranked returning hammer thrower. He might be able to win both national championships next year. What do you think?" I asked.

"How will you be able to balance everything? Do they know you'll have to miss half of the meets because of classes? It's nice that Luis wants you back, but does James?"

"I'm not sure. Probably not. The job isn't even posted yet. I'll apply when it is, and we can see what happens."

"Hi, James. This is Charles. It's about 10:14 a.m. on July sixth. I spoke to Luis the other day, and he shared with me that you might have a throwing coach position posted soon. I'd like to talk to you about that. Please give me a call when you have a moment. Have a great day."

"Hi, James, thanks for taking the time today," I said gleefully. "I appreciate the time."

"Well, there isn't much to discuss today," James said with a sarcastic tone. "You've already heard the news. And Luis spoke to you a few weeks ago, right?"

"Yeah, he called me around the Fourth of July. He said his coach wasn't coming back, and he wanted me to call you. So here we are."

"We received a lot of applications for this position. But Luis insists that we hire you."

"I think I would be a good choice. I'm already familiar with him and Brandon. And from the looks of this past season, the throwing group performed really well. I mean, who wouldn't want to coach a returning All-American? It'd be a great opportunity for anyone."

James and I spoke at great length about the upcoming season. I shared with James my schedule with Fisher and that I would miss half of the meets, but that I wouldn't be missing either indoor or outdoor nationals. I would also be able to attend both the indoor and outdoor Empire 8 conference championship meets. I also shared my thoughts about coaching Luis again, how I would approach the situation with the other athletes, and what our practice schedule would look like.

"Besides Luis," James said, "we have a great group of young throwers coming in. We should have anywhere between ten and fourteen throwers on the team. Can you handle that?"

I remember looking at James with a puzzled look on my face.

"Sure, I had twelve throwers at Fredonia my second year of coaching. We had a strong group, and I was able to have two different practice sessions with the throwers. One session for our more advanced group and a session for our newbies. It made things a lot easier. Everyone was able to get enough reps in, and I was able to give them quality feedback," I said.

"Good, we may have to do that here," James responded. "We won't be practicing in the auxiliary gym anymore. We have outgrown that. We will be throwing in a racquetball court."

"A racquetball court," I said sheepishly. "Is the back wall solid or glass?"

"Glass," James responded.

"OK, that will work. We'll have to be safe and make sure only one person is in the racquetball court at a time."

"You'll also have access to the facility whenever you want. This one court is being reserved for throwers," James said.

"Sounds like a great opportunity. When will you be making a decision?"

James looked at me for what seemed like a couple of minutes. I didn't know what James was thinking. It was an uncomfortable situation.

"To be honest, Charles, I don't think it matters who coaches Luis. I think he'll be successful with anybody as his coach."

*It doesn't matter who his coach is,* I thought to himself. Why would he say that to me if he was going to hire me to be his throwing coach? This is not the way to go about it.

I said, "OK. So you'll let me know in a few days?"

"I can't hire anyone else. I don't think he'll listen to anyone else. I don't think he'll listen to a new college graduate. He trusts and respects you. Do you want the job?" James said.

"Well, that was the most interesting interview I've ever been on," I said to Laura. "James basically told me that Luis will be successful with anyone, and it doesn't matter who his coach is."

"Sounds like a good interview," Laura said with a smile. "Did he offer you the position?"

"He kind of did. After he shared all those thoughts with me he said, 'Do you want the job?'"

"And?"

"I told him that I needed to think about it. I wanted to speak to you first. What do you think? It could be once in a lifetime," I said.

"We've been there. You know there are no guarantees with winning. And why did you tell James that you needed to speak to me first?" Laura asked. "You know you want to take the position."

"I do, but it was what he said that made me a little nervous. He doesn't want me to coach. He offered me the job because Luis wants me to coach. Seems odd to me. James doesn't strike me as someone who would let an athlete or group of athletes call the shots on things like this."

"James knows you are his best option. He could hire a recent graduate, but you both know Luis wouldn't respond to them. He wants you to coach him for a reason. Talk to Luis and see what he says."

I was ready to call Luis when I heard the baby crying on the monitor. I sent Laura a text letting her know I was going up to rock the newest man. Before I went upstairs, I made sure to pick up my coaching journal and pen. I quietly entered the baby's room and picked him up.

"How is my baby boy doing? I hope you didn't have a bad dream, little buddy. I love you with all my heart."

I sat down in the rocking chair and started rocking, one of my favorite parts of being a dad. I began rocking with the baby. Since I had started the doctorate program at Fisher, I had been practicing my rocking and writing skills. As the newest man's little head lay in the crux of my left bicep, I looked down and couldn't help but smile.

"Buddy, I can't believe you are already two months old. It feels like yesterday that we brought home your older brother from the hospital. Now we have you. I love you so much," I whispered. "Thank you."

"Hi, Luis," I said. "I'm sorry I missed your call. I was rocking the newest man."

"I hope I'm not bothering you now, Coach," Luis responded. "How was his nap?"

"A little broken up, but not that bad. I met with James today. We met in the track office for about thirty minutes."

"Well, what did he have to say?"

"James had a lot to say. He shared his concerns with my doctorate program, having to miss half of the meets, and when we would practice. I told him that I had plenty of availability and flexibility with the new job I have. I also told him that we would practice at the normal time, but broken up in a couple of groups. I don't want to have too many athletes practicing at the same time. Especially with that new setup we have. Who knows what might happen if something slips out."

"Did you tell him you'd accept the job?"

"I told James I wanted to wait and discuss the job with you and Laura before I said yes or no."

"Coach, there isn't anything to talk about. Of course I want you to coach me!"

Luis and I spoke on the phone for about an hour. We spoke about Luis's course load, when practice times would be, and how the practice structure would look. I went into great detail about my doctorate program and what that entailed.

"Luis, I'm going to have to miss half of the meets. I'm available for indoor and outdoor nationals, but I won't be able to miss any classes for competitions. I can't afford to take on any more coursework than I'll already have. Does that make sense?"

"Coach, having you there half the time is better than ninety-nine percent of coaches being there all the time. Brandon is excited to have you back too. There are a few other returning throwers, and a lot of freshmen. We'll have a great season together!"

"Let's get together sometime this week for lunch. We can meet where I work and map out the season. We have about eight months to go."

# CHAPTER 40
# ARE YOU READY TO WIN?

I MET LUIS FOR LUNCH ONE AFTERNOON IN EARLY AUGUST before the official start to the 2015–2016 academic year. We met at a local sushi restaurant that we had both enjoyed, and this was the first time we met there together to enjoy the food, but more importantly, to discuss the upcoming season.

"Luis, how is everything going?" I said as I gave Luis a big hug. "How are the last few weeks of the summer treating you?"

"Pretty good, Coach. I just got back from Virginia. I was working on my internship through Wegmans."

"Tell me about that. You were the assistant store manager or store manager, right?"

"Man, Coach, let me tell you. It is so hard to find the right people for the job. Most of July was a mess trying to hire and train people. We would hire one person, and then two would quit. It was horrible."

"But you learned how to run a store?" I said with a smile.

"Coach, I was doing everything. I was supporting the new store manager, I was the front-end manager, I was training people . . . it was a tough summer."

"Are you happy to be back? How many classes are you taking this fall semester?"

Luis took out his computer and shared his course schedule with me. I took out my notebook and wrote Luis's class schedule in his daily planner.

"Looks like you have all afternoon off after two. Did you schedule that on purpose?"

"My senior classes and capstone project courses are all in the morning. I don't have a break until lunch, then one more class, then I'm done at two. I have lots of time to train. And I don't have evening classes either. We have all day to train!"

"This is going to make things much easier, especially through the fall semester. I'm taking a couple of less-demanding courses at Fisher, so we should be able to practice four days a week and get lots of reps in before winter break."

"Coach, you are already talking about winter break. It's still August."

"I know, Luis. I want to make sure our plan for the fall transitions seamlessly into the spring. We really don't have a lot of time to train in the fall."

"Do you know when the official start date of practice is?" Luis asked.

"I don't. I'm guessing the last week of October, like it has been in the past. You have a little over ten weeks of training before the start of the season. That will give us a lot of time to see where you are and how we are going to move forward. How much time did you spend training in Virginia?"

"Not that much. I worked so much that I was able to get to the gym a couple of times a week. I haven't taken a throw since nationals in May."

"Not throwing since May is OK. It's good to give your body a break every once in a while. I'm sure your body will thank you when we really get started in October."

I took out his daily planner and moved it so Luis could see what was written inside.

"Indoor and outdoor nationals are highlighted in green," I said. "We have a long time to train between now and then."

I went into more detail with his calendar.

"The blue-colored weekends are the weekends I'll be able to come to the track meets. The yellow ones mean I have class and won't make it. I already shared all this with James. He knows I will be available for both indoor and outdoor nationals. I won't be able to attend states or ECACs during the indoor season."

"Coach, how are you going to find the time to get all your work done?" Luis asked. "When will you have a break?"

"I don't need a break at this point. Maybe when I graduate I'll take some time off before I start working on another college degree," I said with a chuckle.

When we wrapped up their lunch, Luis and I left with a tentative plan in place. Luis understood that I would not be able to attend every meet. Luis also understood that their practice time would be more meaningful. Meaningful in a deliberate way. A way in which every training session would be documented to ensure the 2015–2016 season would be the best possible season we could produce.

# CHAPTER 41

BEFORE I PULLED OUT OF THE PARKING LOT, I took out my journal. At the top of the page, I wrote *WE*. I knew it was important to talk in terms of *WE*. I remember writing: "Coaching is a joint partnership. A partnership that works because both individuals, the coach and athlete, the dyad, have a common goal. A common purpose. The coach casts the vision for the athlete. The coach is the lightgiver. The person who will illuminate the path brighter than the athlete can illuminate for themselves. The coach and athlete will chart the journey together.

Our 2015–2016 goals:

1. Win the 2016 Division III indoor national championship in the 35-pound weight throw.
2. Win the 2016 Division III outdoor national championship in the hammer throw.

What will it take to win:
Weight throw: 20.00m-plus
Hammer throw: 60m-plus

Luis's current personal best:
Weight throw: 19.16m
Hammer throw: 57.57m
How will we get there:

- Transition technique to toe and two for the weight.
- Transition technique to toe and three for the hammer.
- Track everything—throwing session, weight-room session, rest, recovery, nutrition, and mental preparation."

The thought of setting the course to win not one but two national championships initially seemed daunting. As I pulled out of the parking lot and headed to Fisher for Friday-night class, all I could think about was figuring out a way to get there—to nationals. Getting to nationals wasn't going to be the difficult part. The difficult part was going to be what happens when we get there. I had been to nationals in the past. In my first season at Fredonia, I helped Jen qualify for the 2005 Division III outdoor national championships in the hammer throw.

After our lunch chat in August, Luis began training like I had never seen someone train before. His focus was laser-sharp on winning the 2016 Division III indoor national championship in the 35-pound weight throw. That was his carrot dangling from the imaginary stick he was holding.

Luis was in fantastic shape as the season was about to start. Luis was following a not-so-typical training programming that was created by a throwing coach in the Midwest and had produced excellent results for those throwers who implemented the training philosophy found within the program. Luis agreed to follow the program to a T. When practice officially started at the end of October

2015, Luis was ready to roll.

"All right, Luis. We've been discussing this for a whole summer, and now it is time to begin working on our toe entry for the weight and hammer. This is going to give you the edge you need to get to nationals," I said.

"Coach, I've already been to nationals," Luis quickly responded.

"I know that, but this will give your technique the boost it needs to take you to the next level. This will bring you over 20m (65')," I said.

Similar to what I had done in the past, I gave everyone a marble notebook to keep track of their training. I taught the freshmen what they needed to include in their journal and how to keep track of their weight-room training sessions. I didn't have to do much teaching with our returning group because all but one of the throwers was new to me but experienced in the ways of throwing collegiate implements.

A lot of my training sessions with the advanced group of throwers was focused on throwing. I hung giant whiteboards on one wall of our training facility. Before everyone arrived each day, I would write out their training for the day—what they would be throwing, how many throws, and the weights of the implements. At the beginning of the week, I would ask each thrower to write their top two goals for the week—things they wanted to focus on for that week. Most of our newbies would write things like, "Learn to turn faster," or "Stay in the circle every throw," or "Be able to take two-turn throws and not foul." Our more advanced throwers wrote things like, "Turn more efficiently," or "Generate more speed on my finish," or "Get more comfortable with my technique." Different throwing mindsets, but specific to the individual athletes.

Training went well during our fall semester. We typically

practiced three to four times per week, depending on each athlete's course schedule. Because of the flexibility of my work schedule and Laura's understanding of what this season meant to me, I spent about three hours per day at Nazareth College. I would get there at around 2:30 p.m. and leave close to 5:30 p.m. and be home for dinner by 6:00 p.m. I'd get to my doctorate work after the boys went down for the night, typically around 8:00 p.m.

A lot of what we did in practice was rather mundane and boring. I really wanted to focus on building efficient technique with the throwers, so we did a lot of the same drills over and over and over again. Yes, it was boring. But I knew that boring is what would get our kids where they wanted to go.

# CHAPTER 42
# WHY DO YOU WANT TO WIN?

Before our Thanksgiving break, I met with each thrower individually to discuss goals for the season. Most throwers wanted to throw farther, but their lives outside of training and practice indicated that those were false claims. It took a lot to get under my skin when it came to working with collegiate throwers, but one day a freshman thrower asked me a question, and I responded in a way that they were not expecting. We had a private conversation after practice one November afternoon.

"Coach, we've been doing the same thing for the past couple of months. I don't think I'm getting better," she asked. Let's say her name was Jenna (not really her name; amended to protect her identity).

"Jenna, tell me about that. Why don't you think you are progressing like the others?" I asked.

"I'm not sure. I do the same as everyone else. It hasn't clicked for me yet."

"Well, let me look through your training journal. How are things feeling in the weight room?"

Jenna gave me her notebook. As I flipped through the pages, I realized they were all blank. She hadn't been tracking anything.

"Jenna, you haven't written anything in here. It's tough to tell why you aren't progressing, because there is nothing to talk about."

"Coach, you know I go into the weight room every day after practice. I get my lifting done."

"According to your journal, you haven't done anything. You haven't tracked your rest, recovery, how you are feeling, anything. I don't know why you aren't progressing as much as everyone else. Maybe you don't care that much."

"What do you mean I don't care? I come to practice every day. I care."

"You think you care, but you really don't. You don't care enough to write anything down. It seems like you are just going through the motions. I think if you cared as much as you say you do you'd probably have written something down in your journal."

The more I spoke, the more tears began to flow. I knew I struck a chord with Jenna. She had a lot of talent, but she really didn't care that much. She was barely academically eligible, frequently skipped weight-room sessions, and usually missed a practice or two a week for tutoring. If she did indeed go to tutoring sessions as often as she did, I'd hope she would have better grades.

"Jenna, I think you need to really think about why you want to be a part of this team. If you want to be on the team for the sake of being on the team, that is fine. What isn't fine is to question why you aren't progressing when you haven't taken the time to track anything. I don't know why you aren't progressing, but I can promise that we'll have a more informed conversation once you start writing things down."

Conversations like this weren't typical, but they happened more frequently at Nazareth than they did at Fredonia. Not that it was OK, but I had athletes miss class to attend practice. At Nazareth, I had athletes tell me that they were going to tutoring sessions but weren't going at all. It was one of many different excuses I heard in order to get out of practice. I never threw anyone off a team; I'd let their grades dictate that decision. If an athlete was willing to put in the work, I would meet them halfway and try to get them where they wanted to go. If they put in half the work, it showed in their results.

The goal Luis had for this meet was to hit a throw that would rank him number one in Division III going into the holiday break. We knew it would take a throw around 60', which was not out of the realm of possibility so early in the season. Luis would be unveiling his new technique, and we would use RIT as a canvas to paint our early-season technical prowess on.

"All right, Luis. Let's get a big mark and call it. Slide into that number-one spot before break and put pressure on everyone else in the country," I shared.

"Will do, Coach," Luis responded confidently.

And with one minor technical adjustment between his warm-up and preliminary throws, Luis hit a mark of 59'11.25" in round two to win the meet and beat his teammate Brandon by over 10'. Luis had two throws over 59' and all six throws over 57'. His throws were clustered together, which was good. He didn't hit one big outlier, but rather was consistent and headed into the spring semester as the top-ranked Division III weight thrower.

# CHAPTER 43
# THROWING FANTASY CAMP

THERE WEREN'T AS MANY THROWING-SPECIFIC COACHING conferences held in the Northeast United States in 2016. When I first started coaching at Fredonia in 2004, there were at least two or three conferences held each year in Columbus, Ohio. I would make the trek when I could and spend time learning about the throwing events from Olympians and American record holders like Jud Logan, Lance Deal, Brian Oldfield, and Mac Wilkins.

This throwing-specific coaching clinic at SPIRE took place in early January 2016. I took Luis with me because I felt it important for him to be around other like-minded collegiate and postcollegiate throwers like himself–focused, hungry, and possessing a burning passion and desire for throwing. I also wanted to introduce Luis to Olympians Jud Logan, Lance Deal, Joe Kovacs, Kibwe Johnson, and Reese Hoffa.

While in attendance, Luis hit it off with one of Jud's throwers at Ashland, Jordan Crayon. At this point in his career, Jordan was a multiple-time national champion and All-American thrower in the weight throw and hammer throw. It was my first time meeting

Jordan as well, but I was especially glad Luis and Jordan were able to take some time and talk while we were there.

Both Jud Logan and Lance Deal gave presentations to the attendees. Lance discussed his time as a professional thrower and his experience with finishing second in the 1996 Atlanta Olympic Games in the hammer throw. Lance ended up finishing the 1996 season as the top-ranked hammer thrower in the world. A lot of his talk to the group was centered around building confidence and feeling good about oneself as a thrower. I managed to record a majority of his talk, which I have posted on my YouTube channel. At one point in his presentation, he told everyone to stop recording and shared a personal story of throwing overseas against the best hammer throwers in the world.

Similar to Lance's discussion, Jud spoke about finding a lightgiver—someone who illuminates a path for you brighter than you can illuminate for yourself. He talked a lot about his collegiate coach, how much confidence he had in Jud, and how the impact of his coach's belief in him propelled Jud to throwing at the 1984, 1988, 1992, and 2000 Olympic Games. I had heard Jud speak a few times before this, but this was the first time Jud shared more personal reflections on what it meant to him to have his coach believe in him as much as he did.

By this point in my doctoral journey, I was halfway through the coursework and about a third of the way through my dissertation. If I had attended this conference in January 2015, I'm sure I would have returned to Fisher and changed my dissertation topic. It was at this coaching clinic that I really started thinking more about the dynamics around coach-athlete relationships and how that relationship impacts athlete performances in competition. Lance was an Olympic silver medalist, and Jud was the former American record holder in the weight throw and hammer throw. By their own definitions, they were not great collegiate throwers. It wasn't until later in their collegiate careers that they had found individuals who believed in them so much that they pursued their Olympic dreams.

I knew that great throwers didn't become great by accident. Much like in education, it takes a village to raise a child. I believe the same can be said about athletes—it does indeed take a village, but the right village that fuels the competitive fires that can continue to be pursued past the point that the athlete doesn't think is possible. After Luis and I returned from our one-day conference, I began reviewing the coach-athlete relationship literature to see what I could implement in my daily interactions with my Nazareth athletes that would help me get them where they wanted to go.

## CHAPTER 44

# BEGINNING TO UNDERSTAND THE IMPORTANCE OF COACH-ATHLETE RELATIONSHIPS

After our first meet of the season, I felt 99.9 percent confident that Luis would be returning to indoor nationals. A lot of our planning for our January meets was focused on developing more confidence with his new technique and adding more up-tempo throws early on in the preliminary rounds. We both knew Luis would be making the finals of every meet he competed in, and with me not being able to attend every meet, it gave Luis the opportunity to throw more by feel and be able to self-correct any technical mistakes he thought he was making.

It was during this time in the season that our coach-athlete relationship really began to blossom. I trusted that Luis would follow the plan we laid out for the meets I wasn't able to attend. Luis trusted that I would be able to review the video of his throws and put a plan in place to better move him forward in his journey.

In total, Luis competed in three meets in January 2016. He finished first in all three meets while increasing his seasonal-best throw by over 3'. We knew there wasn't going to be much competition in the area, so in January, our goal was to increase his meet average in each meet. It was a competition within a competition, and one that helped keep Luis focused on the bigger picture while also winning meets by over 10'.

I was not able to attend this early February meet due to being in class. This was Luis's defining early indoor season moment. As I sat in class on Saturday morning, I received a text message from Luis telling me that he didn't feel well and that he didn't want to throw in the meet.

"Coach, I feel horrible. My sinuses are all plugged up. My body's aching all over the place. I think I have the flu," Luis shared via text message.

I stepped out of class and gave him a call.

"Hi, Luis. You looked good yesterday during our premeet practice. What happened? Did you go out last night?" I asked.

"No, I didn't go out, Coach. I think I have a sinus infection or something. I don't think I should throw."

"Luis, nap on the way to Ithaca and let me know how you feel when you get there. I still think you should throw and see what happens."

"I don't want to lose, Coach. I haven't lost all season."

"Luis, I need to get back to class. You don't have to worry about losing. Everyone is trying to catch you. You'll be fine. I know you'll still throw well."

I don't think it was those words of wisdom that propelled Luis on that Saturday afternoon. His body was obviously telling him that he needed a break. I'm glad he was getting sick now and not at nationals. But despite what Luis shared with me on the phone about how he felt, he had the best meet of his career on that day.

Luis ended up throwing the weight a monstrous distance of 65'6.25", or 19.97m. I share the metric mark because the qualifying distance for the USATF indoor national championships for male weight throwers at the time was 20.00m. Luis extended his Division III lead in the weight by over 4' on this day. He called me on the way home from the meet, and even he couldn't believe how well he threw.

"Coach, what happened? I still feel horrible, and I threw really far!"

"Luis, you set all the conference records today. If I'm not mistaken, I think that distance puts you in the top-twenty all-time Division III male weight throwers. This is a huge accomplishment that you should feel really good about! Such an amazing feeling, right?"

"Coach, I'd celebrate tonight, but I'm going to sleep this off. I wonder how far I would have thrown if I felt good."

# CHAPTER 45
# ELEVATING YOURSELF TOWARD GREATNESS

I WAS NOT A FAN OF THE NEW SCHEDULE we had adopted for this season. Our Empire 8 conference championship meet was moved back to align with the states and ECACs. For athletes who were planning on competing at nationals, they had three conference championship meets in a row to compete in beforehand. I didn't think it was fair for the higher-performing athletes in the region to have to compete in three consecutive highly competitive meets before nationals. For teams vying for conference championships, top athletes oftentimes competed in more events than they should have in order to give their teams a chance to win a team championship. Neither the men's or women's programs at the time were considered to win Empire 8 or state championships, but our male throwers had a really good chance of scoring a majority of our team points at both Empire 8s and states.

Although our men scored nineteen out of sixty-four points, I left the meet disappointed. Luis, Brandon, and sophomore Tyler were seeded first, second, and third, respectively. Brandon and Tyler were comfortably seeded second and third. But things did not fall where we had hoped. Luis won, Brandon finished fourth, and Tyler finished sixth. Luis set a championship meet record, throwing 61'9.75". I was more disappointed in myself that I had not prepared everyone else as well as I thought I did. Even Luis looked a little sluggish coming off his illness from the week before.

On Monday at practice, I spoke to Luis, Brandon, and Tyler privately. I shared my thoughts—that I felt they weren't as focused as I thought they should have been and that they had a really good chance to bounce back at the state meet the upcoming week.

At states the following week, Luis had another amazing performance by breaking the championship meet record with a throw of 62'6.75". Luis broke the championship meet record that had stood since 1994, held by my former Fredonia State coach Trevor Hitchcock. Way back in 1994, Trevor threw the weight over 61'. I still get goose bumps thinking about that. Luis was having a phenomenal 2015–2016 season and had just broken a record that had stood for over twenty years. I often wonder what others thought about Trevor when he showed up to competitions. For comparison, Trevor won the 1994 Division III indoor national championship in the 35-pound weight throw with a distance of 61'10". I'm not sure where that would have ranked Trevor all time back then, but his personal best during the 1993–1994 season was 62'10.5".

Due to my class schedule, I was not able to attend either the state or ECAC meet. But at this point in the season, I wasn't offering a lot of technical support. At this point in the season, I believed my role had changed a little bit to offering more emotional support than technical support. Luis had all the physical tools to throw well, but he did sometimes share things with me about his personal life that led me to shake my head in disbelief of what was going on outside of throwing. I thought it was more important to help him block out all the other stuff, and when I was with him to keep his mind focused on throwing and nothing else.

Competing at the ECAC championships held at the Ocean Breeze Athletic Complex on Staten Island, New York, Luis threw the best series of his career. He would go on to win the meet with a throw of 65'1". He had four of five measured throws over 64'. He won the competition by 7'. Luis was going into Division III nationals as the top-ranked men's weight thrower with a seasonal-best throw of 65'6.25".

The nice thing about the week leading up to nationals was that it was our spring break at Nazareth College. There were no other track and field athletes on campus except for Luis, James, and me. We knew that Luis would be throwing at 11:00 a.m. on Friday, March 11. Due to the time difference between throwing in Iowa, we practiced at noon that week to mimic the time he would be throwing at nationals.

It was the most relaxed Luis had ever been. Practice was really laid-back. There wasn't much we could do in a few days that was going to add a lot of distance to his throws. We focused on his technique by working on mimicking his first- and second-round throws at nationals. I spent quite a bit of time telling Luis how proud I was of him, how great all his accomplishments were, and that there was one piece of unfinished business left—indoor nationals.

As I was walking to my car after our Tuesday-afternoon practice, I was flooded with all sorts of emotions. It was finally hitting me that Luis was the top-ranked Division III male weight thrower. He had broken the Empire 8 and state conference records. At this point, I knew it would take a very special athlete to eventually break his school record. Rather than get in my car and drive to work, I took a walk around campus and let all these thoughts settle in my mind. Luis really was the top-ranked thrower. By a wide margin. It was his competition to win. He had the top nine throws in the country leading up to nationals. I was confident in his abilities to throw well at nationals. I felt like I was overthinking the situation. Luis had competed for a majority of the season without me in attendance. Actually, all his best throws came while I was not in attendance. That thought stung a little bit as I made my way to the outdoor track.

Up to this point in the season, this group of male throwers was the best group of collegiate athletes I had ever coached. Brandon and Tyler both threw over 50'. Tyler also scored at ECACs. Tyler would be coming back for his junior season. It was a good situation to be in, but also a bit scary.

# CHAPTER 46
# CEMENTING A LEGACY

DUE TO THE TIME OF THE YEAR, I was not able to travel with Luis and James. They flew out to Iowa on Wednesday morning. I left on Thursday morning. It was a nice trip through Chicago to Iowa City. It wasn't my first time traveling to Iowa. I was returning to Iowa after an eleven-year absence.

James and Luis picked me up, and we went back to the hotel. After I got settled, we took a drive to the indoor complex where the meet would be taking place the following day. Luis took a few throws on Wednesday evening. Just enough to get comfortable in the circle but not enough that they would have a negative impact on the competition in a couple of days. When we did arrive, we found some throwers who took a lot of weight throws. And I mean a lot. I counted one athlete who took fifteen weight throws. We had some weeks that Luis didn't take that many weight throws, let alone the day before the national championship. Luis and I sat in the stands as James went off to talk with other coaches.

"Luis, I don't know what else to say besides how proud I am of you. Look at all you accomplished this season. This has truly been a once-in-a-lifetime season. Tomorrow you can add the icing on the cake," I said confidently.

At the moment, I didn't mean it to sound the way it did. It didn't bother Luis at all. Although he may not have heard me.

"Coach, we are tearing this place up tomorrow. We are going to execute the plan and bring this championship back to Nazareth," Luis said. "I'm ready to compete."

The night before the competition, regional awards were given at a nice dinner hosted by the NCAA and the host college. Due to the lack of tickets—or so Luis and I were told—I was not able to attend. Luis continued to accumulate accolades. He was awarded the best male field athlete of the year for our region. That was not a surprise. Luis was the top-ranked thrower in the country and had not lost a meet all year. His top nine throws were better than the second-ranked men's weight thrower.

The men's weight throw competition began at 11:00 a.m. We arrived at the facility at round 9:00 a.m. Luis needed to be checked in. I shared with Luis that after the check-in time he would be ushered back to a staging room before the start of the competition. It wasn't the first time we had been apart from each other in competition, but it was the first time we would not be able to communicate with each other.

"Luis, take a look around, my friend. How amazing is this? Thank you for letting me tag along on this magical ride," I said. "It has truly been a wonderful experience for me."

"Coach, you did all the work. I'm just throwing far," Luis responded.

After his check-in, Luis and the other fourteen male weight throwers were being called to be brought back into the staging room. Before Luis was taken back, I gave him a big hug and again told him how proud I was of everything he had accomplished so far this season.

As I watched Luis walk away, I turned back to sit down in the coaches area. There was this rectangular box that coaches had to remain in during the competition. I took a seat and reflected on the totality of this season.

I remember thinking about my initial conversation with Luis, my interview with James, and then having lunch with Luis in August 2015. I never asked James why he said it didn't matter who would be coaching Luis—that he would be successful regardless of who was coaching in. It didn't bother me that much over the summer, but it was something I was thinking about now. I remember Dr. Montes shared something in class one evening about the invulnerability of students in school specific to students excelling in class regardless of who their teacher was. At the most critical point in Luis's throwing career, I suddenly had doubts about my skills as a throwing coach.

In the span of approximately three years, Luis had almost doubled his 35-pound weight throw performance. He barely scored at Empire 8s back in 2013. He could barely maintain his composure in the circle as a one-turn thrower. Now I was sitting and taking in the moment of being the coach of the top-ranked weight thrower in Division III. An undefeated weight thrower. A weight thrower who had broken the Empire 8, state, and school records. All this brought tears to my eyes as I thought about what the next couple of hours could mean for Luis. I knew that if he won I was going to call Jud and see what possible next steps could be for a postcollegiate thrower possibly seeking a place to train. At this point, most of the Olympic training centers were still open around the country. I didn't know what the process to gain entry was, but I was going to find out if anyone would be interested in taking on a 20m-plus weight thrower who has unlimited potential and a thirst for learning.

Before I knew it, the throwers were being escorted back into the main complex. I wrote about it earlier, but I can't help but write about it again. There was something different that stuck out about Luis. The way he carried himself—his body language. If I didn't know any better, it seemed as though he had already won the competition. He was walking tall—head up, shoulders back, confident. He had this look on his face that at least told me this competition was over—now please give me my national championship.

In total, there were fifteen throwers competing in the men's weight throw competition. The first flight consisted of seven throwers. The second flight, randomly seeded, consisted of eight throwers. Luis was the fifth thrower of eight in the second flight. Before each flight, they introduced each athlete and any accolades they had earned over the course of the season. The top throw measured from flight one was 61'. A big throw from the flight, considering only one person in the flight had a seed mark over 60'. The thrower who hit 61' in the first flight had a previous best of 59'. He set a personal best over 2' in a major collegiate competition. There were three throwers from flight one who qualified for the finals and earned All-American awards.

A couple of minutes after flight one finished, throwers from flight two were lined up and introduced one by one. When the PA announcer got to Luis, he spoke about him for about thirty seconds. Most other athletes only had their personal-best mark announced. We did not plan what they were going to say for Luis. That information was taken from the NCAA. The PA announcer introduced Luis, shared that he had the top mark entering the competition, was a multiple conference record holder, school record holder, and regional field performer of the year. I couldn't help but smile as the announcer shared all of what Luis had accomplished. He was sharing Luis's accomplishments for this season; however, the foundation for this body of work was started back in 2013. On the surface, it may have looked like he had magically blossomed into a great thrower, but it was all the other "things" that Luis excelled at that brought him to this moment in his life.

Each flight had twenty minutes to warm up before the start of the competition. We kept with our strategy and took three warm-up throws. Our first throw was always to get a feel for the circle; our second throw was more of a tempo, easy rhythm throw; and throw three was an up-tempo 90 percent throw. Luis's first warm-up throw was pedestrian by his standards, just at the 60' line. I thought it looked like a rather easy 60' throw, considering how much adrenaline must have been going through his body. Before he entered the circle for his second throw, I said, "Pick up the pace a bit in two. Get in now!"

Luis unleashed a monster warm-up throw that went well over the 65' line. As it landed, I quickly took a glance around to see if others had witnessed it as well. It was as though all the air left every thrower watching at the same time. You could almost hear a pin drop. Everyone's body language changed. The mood changed. Luis had just woken up everyone in the competition. As he walked out of the circle, he said, "I'm done. Let them catch that."

It was different from our typical strategy, but I wasn't going to say anything to Luis at this point in the competition. Most of the other throwers took a few more throws. One thrower in particular took five warm-up throws. I thought that was a lot, especially since he was going to be taking another three full-effort throws in a few minutes.

Again, we followed the same strategy through the preliminary rounds. After round one, Luis sat in second place to a thrower from Baldwin Wallace. Luis hit a distance of 62'. First place was at 62'3". Luis picked it up in round two with a throw over 63' and took the lead. Luis did not relinquish his lead in the preliminary round of competition.

Luis would be the ninth thrower of nine to throw in the finals. Again, athletes were given fifteen minutes to warm up before the finals. The three throwers from the first flight took advantage of the time. Luis sat in his chair and watched.

I didn't say anything to Luis. He seemed calm and caught up in the moment. He was on the verge of becoming Nazareth College's first track and field national champion. Similar to past meets, the strategy was to extend the lead in round four and put the competition away.

Nobody improved in round four; however, there was something in the air. A couple of throwers were really amped up coming into the finals, but round four saw a lot of foul throws, including Luis's round-four throw. Round five had been our best round of the season. Luis hit some of his best marks in the round. As he stepped into the circle, I said, "Let's bring some heat on this throw. Big push through the finish, Luis!"

And push he did. He unleashed a throw of 67'1.25". A massive personal-best throw. It was at that moment I realized Luis was going to become a national champion. The other throwers would have needed to set personal-best throws over 5' to unseat him. They tried, but nobody was able to catch Luis.

Luis won the 2016 Division III indoor national championship in the 35-pound weight throw. His winning distance landed him sixth all time in Division III. Looking back to last year, Luis had now set a personal-best throw in three consecutive national championship meets. Setting a personal best once or twice is nice, but three consecutive times was out of this world.

I gave Luis a big hug, and with tears in my eyes, I told him that with the exception of my kids being born, this was the most amazing experience of my life. In three short years, Luis went from being a 30' weight thrower to one of the best weight throwers in Division III history. Tradition called for the coach of the winning athlete to distribute the All-American and national championship trophies to the competitors. With tears streaming down my face, I gave Luis his national championship trophy and congratulated him on a remarkable season.

For the remainder of the weekend, Luis was treated like royalty. Athletes from all different event groups congratulated him on his performance. Coaches who I had never spoken to before congratulated me as well.

After his win, I called my wife and shared the news. I talked to both boys and told them that Luis won and that we would be coming home in a couple of days. The boys always asked about Luis. I had the throwers over our house a couple of times that season, and the boys took a liking to Luis. After every practice, they asked me how he was doing, when he would come over again, and if I could call him. He had inadvertently become our third child.

The following day, while Luis and I were watching the shot put competition, I shared my postcollegiate ideas with Luis.

"Luis, welcome to the big time. You broke through the 20m barrier as a Division III thrower. I know it's early, but I think we should discuss next steps on the flight home," I said.

"Coach, I just won. Let's get through the outdoor season first," Luis said with a chuckle. "Let's enjoy this first, then think about the future later."

But I couldn't stop thinking about it. Luis was in rare company. Only one of the top six throwers all time did not go on to throw postcollegiately. The others had found success competing at the USATF indoor national championships, outdoor national championships, and the Olympic Trials. Luis was graduating at the perfect time—2016. He would have a solid quad to build up to the 2020 Olympic Trials. That is all I could think about on the flight back to Rochester.

# CHAPTER 47
# KEEPING THE MOMENTUM GOING

LUIS TOOK THE FOLLOWING WEEK OFF TO RELAX after his indoor season. We didn't have any meets of significance until our outdoor conference meet at the end of April. I knew it would take Luis a couple of weeks to find his hammer rhythm. We didn't put a lot of stock into the first couple of meets of the season. Similar to our indoor campaign, we knew he would qualify for the finals in all his meets, and the way my semester fell at Fisher, I would be able to attend more meets.

A few days after we returned from nationals, I defended my dissertation proposal. By this point in my doctoral journey, I was all-in with my focus on early childhood education, classroom quality, and teacher self-efficacy. I came across an article about teacher efficacy and the relationship between self-efficacy and student outcomes. A lot of the early childhood literature at the time reported that there was a positively significant relationship between preschool teacher self-efficacy, classroom quality, and student outcomes. The results suggested that preschool teachers who feel confident in their abilities to support the academic and social-emotional growth of their students were found to have students who outperformed their peers in math and literacy assessments. I found these outcomes very interesting because a requirement of New York State school's that support universal prekindergarten programming are required to implement a robust data assessment tracking tool that provides evidence of student learning at that age. I incorporated what I had been reading about for the better part of two semesters into my dissertation topic and presented to my committee what I planned on doing for my dissertation.

I enjoyed the structure of my program. Due to the nature of the DEXL program, I was able to select a dissertation topic of my liking and construct a research question around my topic supported by the literature at the time. Looking back, I probably should have been more stressed about coaching, working full-time, taking doctoral classes, and enjoying my time with the boys. I don't know how healthy of a balance it was, but I was still riding my national championships high and aced my presentation. I was one of the first few doctoral candidates in my cohort to defend their proposals. It was a relatively short presentation, no longer than fifteen minutes. I thought it was odd that we only had fifteen minutes to discuss essentially three semesters' worth of work.

As I mentioned, we didn't really have any outdoor meets of note until our conference championships. Besides competing at Empire 8s, I had been pushing James to let me take Luis and Brandon to a track meet at Ashland University.

"James, this will be a great opportunity for Luis and Brandon to compete against higher-quality athletes than what we have been seeing here in Rochester. It'll be a good experience for them to compete against the best Division II throwers in the country," I argued.

"It's a long drive to only compete in the hammer," James responded.

"We'll drive down the night before, compete on Friday, and I will have them back in Rochester late Friday night ready to compete at Fisher on Saturday. We'll make it back–I promise."

It was a tough promise to make. The men's hammer competition began at 2:00 p.m. at Ashland. Ashland is a good six and half hours away from Rochester. I knew that as long as we left by 6:00 p.m. we would be OK. James agreed to let me take Luis and Brandon to Ashland after our Empire 8 meet.

Luis ended up winning the men's hammer championship with a throw of 177'4". It was his worst performance of the season. He won by just over 6'. There really wasn't a concern he was going to win, but there was something going on in his life that I thought was beginning to negatively affect his performances.

After the competition, I asked Luis about it.

"Hey, nice job on completing the three-peat, my friend. You never cease to amaze me," I said.

"Yeah, Coach, this one was close. I won by 6'? I should have broken the meet record," Luis said.

"Well, meet records can be broken. Championships will never be taken away from you. But I'm concerned about you. We've been in a slump for a few weeks. Is everything else OK?" I asked with a concerned look.

"Everything is fine, Coach. I have a lot on my mind," Luis said. "Just lots going on."

# CHAPTER 48

# A SOCIAL LIFE, ACADEMICS, AND THROWING—YOU CAN ONLY BE GREAT AT TWO

By the look on his face, I knew he didn't want to share anything with me, which was fine. I was concerned that whatever else was going on outside of track was hurting his performances. I was expecting personal-best throws right out of the gate, but his performances weren't much better than his sophomore season. He was throwing in the mid- to upper 180s pretty much all season and then dipped under 180' for the first time. I wasn't concerned that he wasn't going to qualify for nationals. I knew his throw would come. I thought it would come at Ashland University.

The drive into Ashland was wonderful. I had visited plenty of times over the years, but it had been a while since I had been on campus. Traveling to this meet was just as important to me as it was to Luis and Brandon. I always enjoyed talking to Jud. He had this gift of speaking to someone and making them feel like they were the most important person in the world at the time. It was something about those piercing blue eyes he had that made you feel like you were the only person around.

I think Luis got a kick out of how I always got excited when I either talked about Jud or was in his presence. At the time, I considered Jud to be the top American throwing coach. Up until that point in his coaching career, Jud had coached over two hundred All-Americans and over forty national champions. Remarkable numbers from someone at a small private Division II university that did not offer a lot in the ways of athletic scholarships. But whatever Jud touched turned into gold. Or in his case, those he worked with developed into All-Americans.

For reasons I'll discuss in a moment, Luis picked this meet to have his worst throwing performance since his freshman year. Luis finished eighth in the hammer with a throw of 167'2". He didn't qualify for the finals. He was devastated.

After the competition, Jud spoke privately with Luis. I'm not sure what he said, but I didn't think it was appropriate to ask. We grabbed dinner in Ashland and were on the road back to Rochester by 7:00 p.m. For whatever reason, Brandon immediately fell asleep in the back seat. With Brandon snoring away, it was a good time to have a conversation with Luis.

"What do you think about today, Luis? Tell me about your performance," I said, as caring as possible. "What happened?"

"I don't know, Coach. It was a bad day," Luis said.

"Luis, I've known you for almost four years. You don't just have bad days like this. I think something else is going on. Is there anything you want to talk about?"

"No, Coach. Everything is fine."

"OK, I understand that you don't want to share anything with me. That is fine. I just want to tell you that you have an amazing opportunity sitting in front of you. You have a chance to win both the hammer and weight championships in the same season. You really are on the cusp of greatness. I don't want anything outside of track to take that possibility away from you. You don't have to tell me, I respect that. But think about the next month of the season. Whatever is bugging you is negatively affecting your performances."

Luis didn't say a word from Mentor, Ohio, until we passed Erie, Pennsylvania, on I-90 East. I was singing along to the oldies radio station I found. Luis was staring out the window. Then he finally opened up.

"I'm having some issues with this girl," he said embarrassingly. "We are on and off. When we are on, everything is great. Right now we are off," he said.

"OK, was it a mutual decision to be off right now?"

"She wanted to be off, Coach. She said she needed a break. But then I found out she was messing around with other guys."

Luis thought he was in a difficult situation. I had to be very careful with how I responded because we had a track meet to compete in in less than twelve hours. I didn't want to derail the rest of his outdoor season.

"Well, if she wanted to take a break, then it's probably a good idea to respect her wishes. Why does it bother you that she is with other guys? Nazareth has plenty of girls on campus. Like you always told me before, try to find your next ex," I said with a chuckle. It even got a laugh out of Luis.

For the better part of the next couple of hours, we discussed his relationship and how it was affecting his performances.

"Luis, I'm not a relationship expert. It sounds like she isn't interested in you right now. And that is OK."

"Coach, she is messing around with other guys."

"That is her decision. You can't decide that for her. You can control your decisions and your emotions. Right now your emotions are all over the place. They are wreaking havoc on your outdoor season. Let's try to move past this first month of the season and start over tomorrow at Fisher."

I shared some focus strategies I had been reading about in my nonexistent free time. I told Luis that it was important for him to block out the outside stuff going on in his life by enjoying the moment at practice and at meets. We talked about being fully engaged in what was happening at meets in an attempt to distract the mind away from everything else that was happening. I didn't know if anything was sinking in or not. I had my share of relationship issues in the past as well. I could empathize with what he was experiencing. Our conversation made the rest of the drive pass quickly. And before we knew it, I was pulling into Nazareth College, just before 1:00 a.m.

"OK, guys, I'll meet you at Fisher by eight. Please make sure you set your alarms. I'll give you both a call at seven."

## CHAPTER 49

# FOUR NATIONAL CHAMPIONSHIPS, FOUR PERSONAL-BEST THROWS

LUIS ENDED UP TURNING THINGS AROUND the last few meets of the season. He set a seasonal-best throw at Fisher the following day, throwing the hammer 187'6". Luis followed up that win with a win at the outdoor state championship meet. On May 6, 2016, Luis set a personal best with a winning throw of 193'1". He won the state championship by less than 2', again beating out a tough group of throwers from RPI.

Luis suffered his first loss of the season at ECACs. About ten days from outdoor nationals, Luis finished second with a throw of 188'1". He was still throwing within 95 percent of his personal-best performance, but his performances were all over the place. Even with how diligently Luis kept track of everything, it was difficult to predict how he was going to throw. I wasn't able to make the trip out to ECACs. Luis called me while I was on break from class.

"Coach, not good today. I finished second. I should have won, but I didn't have it today," Luis said.

"Luis, it's OK. From what I saw online, your throws were consistent. We didn't have a range buster. How do you feel?"

"I feel good, but my mind hurts. I should have won."

"I can tell you sound disappointed. You've had a busy couple of weeks. Enjoy the ride home. You'll graduate tomorrow and then can put all your time and energy into this push toward nationals."

Similar to the indoor season, I was not able to travel with James and Luis to Iowa. With the men's hammer competition taking place on the twenty-eighth, I traveled on the twenty-sixth. Luis again was awarded regional field performer of the year. He defended his state and Empire 8 conference championships, set a personal best in the process, and broke the Empire 8 conference record in the hammer.

I felt really good about his chances to win the hammer championship. Even though the last few weeks of the season were not to our liking, I believed in Luis and that he would find a way to pull out a win.

Luis was throwing in flight two of the hammer competition. And again, similar to the indoor competition, there were three throwers from flight one who qualified for the finals. Before the weather turned, Luis hit another personal best in round three of the prelims. He hit a mark of 194'6". It came just in time too. As Luis was walking out of the circle after his third-round throw, the heavens opened up, and it started raining. Only a couple of throwers improved their marks in the finals. Unfortunately, Luis was not one of them. Luis finished third in the competition with a throw of 194'6". It was his fourth consecutive national championship meet in which he set a personal best.

"Luis, I am so proud of you. Another personal best. Another All-American award," I said in excitement. "How do you feel?"

"I feel good, Coach. I thought there was another one in there. We'll get that big throw next year," Luis said confidently.

"Yes, we will, Luis. Indeed we will."

# Part III

# CHASING DREAMS

# CHAPTER 50
# GRADUATE SCHOOL AND PROFESSIONAL THROWING

THE STRENGTH OF THE COACH-ATHLETE RELATIONSHIP is a predictive factor of athlete performance (Infurna, 2022). Much has been said over the past three decades in the literature focused on coach-athlete relationships focused on predictive factors of athletic performance. A primary indicator of the strength of the coach-athlete relationship has been found to be trust (Infurna, 2023). I believe that much of Luis's success can be boiled down to how we trusted each other over the course of our relationship.

After Luis graduated from Nazareth College, he was accepted into the human resource management MBA program at Nazareth College. Luis would be sticking around for another year. Another year to work together toward accomplishing new goals and climbing a new Mount Everest. The 2020 Olympic Trials could be found at the peak of this new Everest. With four years to train, or so we thought at the time, we both believed that Luis would have been able to qualify for the 2020 Olympic Trials in the hammer throw.

It was not surprising to me that I was able to watch Luis grow, mature, and develop into a very successful postcollegiate thrower. To help support him in this endeavor, I registered a track and field club through USATF to help support Luis and other postcollegiate throwers who might have been overlooked—the "sleeper" throwers.

Luis continued to train at Nazareth College for the 2016–2017 season. Along the way, we began coaching local high school throwers who were also flying under the radar. Luis helped me coach local talent while I continued to coach him.

Our world is built upon relationships. The stronger the relationship two individuals share, the more opportunities those individuals have to grow and support each other. At the time, I believed my relationship with Jud at Ashland was pretty good. To better give Luis a chance to achieve his throwing goals, I encouraged Luis to contact Jud to see if he could travel to Ashland every once and a while to train with Jud's postcollegiate group.

"Coach, Jud won't let me train out there. I'm an outsider. He won't take me," Luis said.

"You may be an outsider," I began, "but you are also a sleeper, raw talent. Jud will be able to mold you into a more efficient and powerful thrower. Ask him to go out and train every once in a while. The worst he can say is no," I said.

After a couple of meets early in the winter of 2016 and 2017, Luis did in fact have a conversation with Jud about traveling to Ashland to train. Jud had a strong training group at the time, Jordan Crayon and Megan Tomei leading the way. Both Ashland graduates, but more importantly, both of them had a relationship with Luis. After competing at Ohio State in early 2017, Luis started traveling to Ohio a couple of times a month to train with Jordan and Megan, while also competing in various meets across Ohio.

In one of those Ohio meets, Luis ended up throwing over 21m and qualified for the USATF indoor national championships. With the hectic nature of my work schedule, I was not able to travel to those meets with Luis. In 2017 Luis finished sixth at the USATF Indoor National Championships with a throw of 72'2.50 in the sixth round. It was his fifth consecutive national championship meet in which Luis set a personal best.

I was helping him as much as I could, but I knew there was only so far I could take Luis in Rochester without a strong training group to support his growth. After another successful 2018 indoor campaign, with a seventh-place finish at the USATF Indoor National Championships, Luis continued to grow as a thrower, and just when he was getting ready to graduate with his MBA, I asked him if he thought about moving to Ashland to train on a full-time basis with Jud.

## CHAPTER 51

# THE ANSWER IS ALWAYS NO IF YOU DON'T ASK

I PLANTED THIS SEED IMMEDIATELY after Luis won the 2016 Division III indoor national championship in the weight throw. I knew he was primed to move and join a group of throwers who would help him reach greater heights. Luis attended a training camp of sorts in June 2018 hosted by Ashland University. While there, Jud and Luis engaged in a conversation about moving to Ashland to train. Luis called me with the news.

"Coach, Jud just asked me if I wanted to join his training group in Ashland," he said. "You were right—I just needed to find the right place and time."

"Luis, you still have so much potential. Jud is going to squeeze every last bit of potential out of you," I said. "This is an amazing accomplishment. Jud doesn't take just anyone—this is a big deal."

And indeed it was a big deal. A big deal for us. Certainly for me. Luis would be the second thrower I'd be sending to train with Jud. I believed this was in part due to the relationship I had with Jud.

I respected and admired Jud. If Jud didn't think anything of me, I don't think Luis would have been invited. Maybe he would have, but it would have been more difficult to open that door. Shortly after Luis graduated, he packed up everything he had and moved into a small apartment in Ashland, Ohio. He had secured a job in the admissions office as well. Luis would be able to train with arguably the best throwing coach in the world every single day. I may have been more excited than he was.

It is difficult to put into words how this experience affected me as a coach. In only a few years, Luis had developed into an up-and-coming postcollegiate hammer thrower. His weight throw personal best of 72'2.50" set the Puerto Rican national record. He was invited to go train at Ashland University with Jud Logan. Jud did not just take any throwers to join his group. I knew that. Luis knew that. And social media knew that. It may have created a small ripple in the throwing waters because Jud was essentially accepting an outsider into his group, his family.

I remember watching the Olympic Trials as a college student and learning about Calvin and Alvin Harrison, twins who lived in their car for a couple of years just so they could train with the Santa Monica Track and Field Club. They gave up their lives in order to have a chance of climbing Everest. Minus the living in his car situation, Luis gave up everything in Rochester to pursue this path. I don't think it was a tough decision for Luis. We both understood what this meant. I didn't mind Luis moving away. It was time. I believe I had taken him as far as I could, and now it was time for Jud to work his magic and see if Luis would be able to qualify for the Olympic Trials. Other postcollegiate throwers were accepted into Jud's throwing family in the early 2000s: A. G. Kruger, Kibwe Johnson, Derek Woodske, Joe Woodske, and Crystal Smith. They all qualified for international teams. A. G. gave up everything out West and drove to Ashland without a job or place to live, but he brought a dream with him. They all had dreams. Luis was pursuing his dream!

In the summer of 2019, Luis hit a monster personal-best throw of close to 230' in the hammer. Luis was making huge gains in the hammer. Whenever I spoke to Luis, he had this excitement about him. At this point in his career, I likened Luis's career to those that were talked about on television during the Olympic Trials. Others who were highlighted oftentimes had stories of traveling many miles with no guarantees of success, but they still made the decision to do so.

But with all great things, the drive for the Olympic Trials came to a halt. As the world shut down in the spring of 2020, so did the dream of pushing forward toward the Olympic Trials. It was at this point in Luis's life that he had a decision to make. Luis was still climbing the ranks of American hammer throwers; however, the instability of lacking a stable career was starting to creep up on him.

Luis and I spoke quite often about the decision to put off the dream of the Olympic Trials and "retire." Maybe not officially, but take time away and get things settled with his career.

In 2020 Luis moved to North Carolina to pursue his career in human resource management and put his MBA to good use. Since joining ADP, Luis has found new successes, becoming eligible for the company's prestigious president's club honor in his second full year of employment. I was sad when Luis shared the news with me that he would be moving away from throwing. I knew this time would come at some point. The Ashland dream lasted two years. Luis improved both his weight and hammer distances in his two years working with Jud.

I often wonder what might have happened in the spring and

summer of 2020. Would one more year have been enough? How close could Luis have gotten to competing at the Olympic Trials?

# CHAPTER 52
# MY PROUDEST COACHING MOMENT

In July 2022, I received a call from James telling me that Luis would be inducted into the Nazareth College Sports Hall of Fame that fall. I was ecstatic to hear that Luis would be inducted! James also shared with me that Luis requested me to induct him in the HOF.

"Laura, I just got off the phone with James," I said.

"What did he have to say?" Laura asked.

With tears in my eyes, I shared the news with Laura. "Luis is going to be inducted into the HOF in September! Luis requested that I induct him," I said. "I can't believe it's finally happening, Laura!"

"You should be proud of yourself," said Laura. "After all the two of you went through over his four years at college, you should feel good about it. You earned it too."

We began talking about what I should say or share at the HOF ceremony. There are plenty of stories I can share about Luis. The first time we met, his freshman season, the teardrop muscle story, traveling to Boston, attending the coaching conference at SPIRE, going to nationals, etc. The more we talked about it, the more emotional I began to feel.

"Laura, I don't know if I'll make it through my speech. What if I start crying?"

"You probably will start crying. Look at yourself right now. You can't get through a memory without more tears and laughter."

The day had finally arrived. I couldn't wait to induct Luis into the HOF. Even after three months, I hadn't prepared a formal speech. I wrote down some notes on a piece of paper, but I didn't know if reading from those notes would be appropriate considering the moment.

"Coach, it's so nice to see you," said Luis with his arms outstretched.

It had been over two years since Luis and I had spent any time together. I visited Luis in Ohio during the COVID-19 pandemic, but I hadn't seen him since.

"Coach, are you ready?" asked Luis.

"Like the time we drove to Ohio State ready," I replied. "Luis, you look amazing. Ready to take a couple of throws after this?"

"I'm not in that kind of shape tonight, Coach. Did you write anything down for tonight?"

"I have a couple of things written down, but I don't think I'll be able to read from my notes."

Luis was joined by his college sweetheart, Kati. Luis's dad and stepmom also attended the ceremony. It was held in an auditorium on Nazareth's campus. It was a relaxed setting, with no formal seating arrangements or dinner. It was a laid-back atmosphere.

"I mean, they could have held this in a nicer setting," I chuckled. "They could have hosted the dinner and ceremony in the field house. It may have been a more appropriate setting."

"Coach, come on now. It doesn't matter, does it? At this point, it's great to be here and to spend time with you and my parents," said Luis.

Luis, Kati, James, Luis's family, and I sat together during dinner. Besides Luis, there were six additional individual athletes inducted and two teams of distinction. At Luis's request, I would be inducting him into the HOF. Prior to this induction, the assistant athletic director would have the honor of preparing a brief biography of each athlete and induct the athlete into the HOF.

"We normally do not have someone else induct athletes into the HOF. In previous years, our ceremony has dragged on, but at Luis's request, I'd like to introduce Dr. Charles Infurna. Dr. Infurna was Luis's throwing coach while a student-athlete. Please help me welcome Dr. Charles Infurna."

My heart was pounding through my neatly pressed white dress shirt. I was used to speaking to large groups, but this occasion was different. A sense of excitement and a rush of emotions flooded my mind as I walked up to the podium. Even at the eleventh hour, I had not prepared a formal speech. I knew I had only a couple of minutes, but I wanted to make the best of the time to introduce Luis and induct him into this very special fraternity and sorority of graduates from Nazareth College.

"It is my extreme pleasure to be speaking with you tonight," I said nervously. "In all honesty, Luis probably shouldn't be here. Not competing in track and field in high school, Luis was discovered in our cafeteria a couple of months before the season started. When I first met with James for my interview, he told me that I would be working with two freshmen male athletes and one senior female thrower. Luis and I didn't initially hit it off. Luis ran into some academic troubles, dropped a course during the first week of practice, and instantly became ineligible to practice because he fell below the required twelve credit hours."

At this point in my speech, I took two deep breaths. At this moment, while I took a sip of water from the bottle I brought up to the podium with me, I made eye contact with Luis's dad in the crowd. Again, I felt an overwhelming sense of emotions run through me. The glance with Luis's dad might have lasted only a second, but it seemed like an eternity to me. Tears began to slowly cascade down my face. I took an additional breath and continued.

"I never thought I would see Luis again. I didn't expect to, because he had no ties to track and field. It wasn't a sport he competed in while in high school, and nothing was holding him to our team. But Luis was different. That is why I'm inducting him tonight. We remained in constant contact over the course of that fall semester. I would share weight-room workouts with Luis, and he would message me back his thoughts about how things were going. I sent him some videos to watch on YouTube, but I didn't know if he would do the work while he was waiting to come back in January."

Again, I had to take a deep breath before I lost composure in front of the crowd sitting and standing before him. I took another quick sip of water before continuing my speech.

"Luis rejoined our team in January 2013. He was ready! He took our practices seriously and paid close attention to what I was asking him and his teammates to do. In his first meet, Luis threw the weight about 30'. It wasn't a great start, but there were glimpses of what was to come."

At this point in my speech, I could no longer maintain my composure. The tears began streaming down my face. My voice became broken and muffled. I knew I had to wrap up this speech before I lost total control of my emotions.

"After that first meet in January 2013, I think things worked out pretty well for us," I said with a chuckle. Some in the audience laughed as well, considering the importance of this moment. I continued, "Luis threw about 35' farther over the course of his career, finishing his throwing career ranked as the number six all-time DIII weight thrower with a mark of 67'2". It is my great honor and pleasure to induct Luis Rivera into Nazareth College's Athletic HOF."

"Thank you for this opportunity, Luis," I whispered in Luis's ear as we hugged onstage. "Thank you."

# APPENDIX

## LUIS RIVERA'S COLLEGE AND POSTCOLLEGIATE THROWING CAREER HIGHLIGHTS

- 2016 Division III Indoor National Champion in the 35-pound weight throw
- Number six all time in Division III weight throwers with a distance of 67'1.25"
- 2016 Division III Northeast Region Indoor Field Performer of the Year
- Four-time All-American (two-time 35-pound weight and two-time hammer throw)
- Empire 8 Conference record holder in the 35-pound weight throw and hammer throw (194'6")
- Six-time Empire 8 conference champion (three indoors and three outdoors)
- Three-time state champion
- Two-time ECAC champion
- 2017 and 2018 USATF Indoor National Championship participant
- Weight throw personal best of 22.02m
- Hammer throw personal best of 68.77m
- Puerto Rican national record holder in the 35-pound weight throw

# BIBLIOGRAPHY

Bennie, A., & O'Connor, D. (2012). "Coach-athlete relationships: A qualitative study of professional sport teams in Australia." *International Journal of Sport and Health Science*, 10, 58–64.

Deci, E. L., & Ryan, R. M. (2000). "The 'what' and 'why' of goal pursuits: Human needs and the self-determination of behavior." *Psychological Inquiry*, 11, 227–268.

Gould, D., Collins, K., Lauer, L., & Chung, Y. (2007). "Coaching life skills through football: A study of award-winning high school coaches." *Journal of Applied Sport Psychology*, 19, 16–37.

Harry, M., & Weight, E. (2021). "Post-collegiate athlete transitions and the influence of a coach." *Journal for the Study of Sports and Athletes in Education*, 1–26.

Infurna, C. J. (2023). "The heart of the matter: High-performance athletes' perceptions of the coach-athlete relationship." *Techniques Magazine*, May (4).

Infurna, C. J. (2022). "Sustained success at the Olympic level: Perspectives on coach-athlete relationships from track and field throwing coaches." *Track Coach*, Winter (238).

Jowett, S., & Shanmugam, V. (2016). "Relational coaching in sport: Its psychological underpinnings and practical effectiveness." In R. Schinke, K. R. McGannon, & B. Smith (Eds.). *Routledge International Handbook of Sport Psychology* (471–85). London. United Kingdom: Routledge.

Jowett, S., & Nezlek, J. (2011). "Relationship interdependence and satisfaction with important outcomes in coach-athlete dyads." *Journal of Social and Personal Relationships*, 29, 287–301.

Jowett, S., & Poczwardowski, A. (2007). "Understanding the coach-athlete relationship." In S. Jowett, & D. Lavallee (Eds.), *Social Psychology in Sport* (3–14). Champaign, IL: Human Kinetics.

Jowett, S., & Chaundry, V. (2004). "An investigation into the impact of coach leadership and coach-athlete relationship on group cohesion." *Group Dynamics: Theory, Research, and Practice*, 8, 302–11.

Jowett, S., & Cockerill, I. M. (2003). "Olympic medalists' perspective of the athlete-coach relationship." *Psychology of Sport and Exercise*, 4, 313–31.

Keegan, R. J., Harwood, C. G., Spray, C. M., & Lavallee, D. (2014). "A qualitative investigation of the motivational climate in elite sport." *Psychology of Sport and Exercise*, 15, 97–107.

Lafreniere, M. A. K., Jowett, S., Vallerand, R. J., & Carbonneau, N. (2011). "Passion for the coaching and the quality of the coach-athlete relationship: The mediating role of coaching behaviors." *Psychological Sport Exercise*, 12 (2), 144–52.

Mageau, G. A., & Vallerand, R. J. (2003). "The coach-athlete relationship. A motivational model." *Journal of Sports Science*, 21 (11), 883–904.

Potrac, P., Jones, R., & Armour, K. (2002). "'It's All About Getting Respect': The coaching behaviors of an expert English soccer coach." *Sport, Education and Society* 7 (2), 183–202.

Powers, M., Fogaca, J., Gurung, R. A. R., & Jackman, C. M. (2020). "Predicting student-athlete mental health: Coach-athlete relationship." PSI CHI, The International Honor Society in Psychology, 25(2), 172–180.

Rezania, D., & Lingham, T. (2009a). "Coaching IT project teams: A design toolkit." *International Journal of Managing Projects in Business* 2 (4), 577–90.

Simons, E. E., & Bird, M. D. (2022). "Coach-athlete relationship, social support, and sport-related psychological well-being in National Collegiate Athlete Association Division I student-athletes." *Journal for the Study of Sports and Athletes in Education*, 1–20.

# ACKNOWLEDGMENTS

**To all the athletes I've coached over the course of my career,** thank you for letting me be a small part of your lives and entrusting me with the opportunity to help you achieve your goals and aspirations. I'd especially like to thank my first core group of athletes at SUNY Fredonia—Jen, Meredith, Nick, and Tim. I wasn't a very good coach back then, but thank you for letting me learn alongside you for two years.

**To my parents, Anna and Giuseppe,** thank you for your unconditional love and support. I know I will always be able to count on you through the good times and bad. I love you.

**To my brother Frank,** thank you for always taking the time to take a call, listen to my crazy and outlandish ideas, and support my out-of-the-box endeavors. Everyone deserves to have a brother like you. I love you.

**To Jud Logan.** Coach Logan, I hope this book makes you proud. You probably never realized that you were my lightgiver. You welcomed me into the Ashland family without hesitation, and I am forever grateful to you for everything you did to support my coaching career and the support you provided Jen and Luis as they continued pursuing their throwing dreams.

**To Luis Rivera,** this book would not have been possible without your grit, determination, open-mindedness, and motivation to reach your fullest potential. I cannot share with you enough how proud I am of you and all that you have accomplished in your professional and throwing careers. Your eagerness to persist in your quest for greatness is a true testament to the work ethic you possess as you continue to accomplish all the goals you set for yourself.

**To Dan Chambliss.** Thank you for your willingness to meet with me eight years ago. I appreciate your friendship, mentoring, and time to listen to all of my crazy ideas. You have always been supportive of my writing endeavors, and I am forever indebted to you for writing the foreword to this book.

**To James Goss.** Thank you for taking a chance on me back in 2012 and again in 2015. This book would not have been possible without your understanding and commitment to give me a chance to coach again after time away.

**To Tim Giagios.** Thank you for your unwavering friendship over the past two decades. You welcomed me into the Alfred State track and field family without hesitation in 2020. It has been an exhilarating experience these past six years.

**To Paul Csont.** Coach Csont, what a wild ride we were on back in the early 2000s. You were the one constant motivating presence during my time as an athlete and then assistant coach at SUNY Fredonia. Without your persistence and encouragement, I would have never accepted the assistant coaching position in 2004–05. Thank you!

**To Ed Jaskulski.** Ed, you are one of the most knowledgeable coaches I know. Thank you for always allowing me to share training and coaching ideas with you. You never shy away from conversations about how we as coaches can enhance the experiences of our athletes. Thank you for your friendship dating back to our competitive days in the early 2000s. I appreciate all that you have done to help support my coaching and writing career!

**To Adarian Barr.** Coach Barr, without realizing it, you started shaping my philosophy of coaching before I ever entertained the idea of coaching. You brought to light the importance and impact a positive coach-athlete relationship can have on an athlete. You brought out the very best in me as an athlete, but it was those car-ride conversations that began shaping my philosophy on coaching. You inspired me then, and you continue to inspire me now after that one magical season we had at SUNY Fredonia together!

# ABOUT THE AUTHOR

Dr. Charles J. Infurna is a dynamic and energetic speaker and coach who has dedicated his research and coaching career toward unraveling the intricacies of interpersonal dynamics in the world of sport.

His research delves into the profound impact of coach-athlete relationships on athletic performance and athlete well-being. His work has provided practical insights for coaches and athletes looking to enhance the quality of their relationships. Through his publications, presentations, and collaborations with sports organizations, Dr. Infurna continues to shape the landscape of coach-athlete relationship research, empowering coaches and athletes alike to cultivate meaningful connections and achieve their highest potential in sport and life.

Dr. Infurna holds an EdD in executive leadership from St. John Fisher University and an advanced degree in school building leadership, a graduate degree in curriculum and instruction, and an undergraduate degree in childhood education from the State University of New York at Fredonia.

He grew up in Rochester, New York, and now lives in Almond, New York, with his four inquisitive and energetic boys—Joseph, Dominic, Santino, and Roman.